AUBURN AND PLACER COUNTY

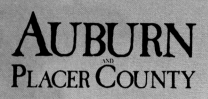

AUBURN AND PLACER COUNTY

**Crossroads of a
Golden Era
A. Thomas Homer**

"Partners in Progress"
by Betty Roby

Produced in cooperation
with the Auburn Area
Chamber of Commerce

Windsor Publications, Inc.
Northridge, California

Windsor Publications, Inc.—History Books Division

Editorial Director: Teri Davis Greenberg
Director, Corporate Biographies: Karen Story
Design Director: Alexander D'Anca

Staff for *Auburn and Placer County: Crossroads of a Golden Era*
Manuscript Editor: Nora Perren
Photo Editor: Laura Cordova
Assistant Director, Corporate Biographies: Phyllis Gray
Editor, Corporate Biographies: Brenda Berryhill
Production Editor, Corporate Biographies: Una FitzSimons
Senior Proofreader: Susan J. Muhler
Editorial Assistants: Didier Beauvoir, Thelma Fleischer, Alyson Gould, Kim Kievman, Michael Nugwynne, Kathy B. Peyser, Pat Pittman, Theresa Solis
Sales Representative, Corporate Biographies: Carter Reynolds
Art Director: Christina Rosepapa
Layout Artist, Corporate Biographies: Mari Catherine Preimesberger
Layout Artist: Tanya Maibroda
Designer: Thomas Prager

Library of Congress Cataloging-in-Publication Data
Homer, A. Thomas, 1943–
    Auburn and Placer County: crossroads of a golden era/A. Thomas Homer: Partners in progress by Betty Roby.—1st ed.
    "Produced in cooperation with the Auburn Area Chamber of Commerce."
    Bibliography: p. 133
    Includes index.
    1. Auburn (Calif.)–History. 2. Placer County (Calif.)–History. 3. Auburn (Calif.)–Description–Views. 4. Placer County (Calif.)–Description and travel–Views. 5. Auburn (Calif.)–Industries. 6. Placer County (Calif.)–Industries. I. Roby, Betty. II. Auburn Area Chamber of Commerce. III. Title.
F869.A9H66   1988   979.4'38–dc19   88-5640
ISBN: 0-89781-237-9   CIP

Windsor Publications, Inc.
Elliot Martin, Chairman of the Board
James L. Fish, III, Chief Operating Officer
Hal Silverman, Vice-President/Publisher

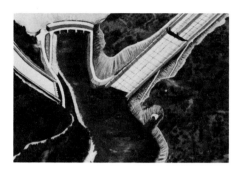

Contents

Dedicated to my children, Melissa and Kim,
knowing that our past only has a future in our young.

Acknowledgments

History can be described in two ways. The first can be found on the pages of books that record the events of an era. Auburn and Placer County have been the focus of countless books, magazine articles, and newspaper stories. Particularly helpful were the *Auburn Journal,* the *Placer Herald,* the *Colfax Record,* and *Sierra Heritage Magazine.*

In addition, the Placer County Historical Society, the Placer County Museum, and the Auburn-Placer County Library must be singled out for continuing to make certain our history remains an important part of our community.

Secondly, the most interesting aspect of any historic research is the people who lived the history we read about today. It would be difficult to list all of these individuals and their contributions. A few, however, must be mentioned by name. The first is my friend and fellow Auburn Host Lions Club member John Robinson. John's love and respect for Auburn and its residents is evident in his every action. A former assistant postmaster, John saw Auburn grow throughout the twentieth century. Mel Locher and Floyd J. Locher have also proven to be men who share a love and respect for this community that is reflected in their efforts to share our history with all those wanting to take the time to listen. May W. Perry spent many years collecting history about our community and working to preserve it for all of us.

This book would not have become a reality if not for the enthusiasm of Auburn Area Chamber of Commerce Executive Director Bruce Cosgrove. Writers write for the love of the subject matter. Editing their words, on the other hand, is often difficult and requires patience and skill. Kathleen Harris Haupt grew up in Placer County and Applegate. Her knowledge of the area and her editing skills have contributed to the success of this project.

Facing page: Clouds hover over Lake Tahoe. Photo by John Elk III

Above: Winter snow melts into the Yuba River. Photo by A. Thomas Homer

Introduction

It is difficult to separate this place we call Auburn and Placer County from the people and events that not only shaped our own community, but also changed the history of this nation. Auburn began as a peaceful place where Indians hunted along the rivers and lived untouched by the outside world for centuries.

Gold brought miners and miners brought changes beyond anyone's dreams. The discovery of gold in 1848 brought this region to the attention of the world. Early settlers arrived on foot, by horseback, and in wagons. Along with the miners who were looking for quick profit came those people who wanted to settle the region. Small towns began to spring up throughout the western foothills of the Sierras. Some soon disappeared into the landscape. Others, like Auburn, became the center of political and social happenings.

When gold became harder to find, the Central Pacific Railroad began its eastward march over the Sierras to make the American dream of a transcontinental railroad from the east coast to the west coast a reality. The most difficult stretch on which to build a railroad was between Sacramento and Truckee, through the heart of Placer County. Just like the discovery of gold, the building of the railroad meant major changes in Placer County. The routes for east-west travel switched from the railroad to highways, and again Placer County was the place Interstate 80 was built.

Throughout the 136-year history of Placer County, many changes occurred because of the discovery of gold, the building of the railroad, its rich agricultural heritage, and its many major highways. Yet the people of Auburn and Placer County continue to reflect the values first brought to this area by early pioneers.

Written for people who want to know more about this fascinating community and how it all began, this book is a historical account of Placer County people and the events they helped to shape.

A. Thomas Homer
Auburn, California

Facing page: California poppies blanket the Sierra foothills.
Photo by John Elk III

9

Chapter
I

The Foothills Wilderness

Pre-1848

A walk along old abandoned trails hidden from view by age, nature, and the changing fortunes of man begins to tell the story of life in Auburn and in Placer County before the discovery of gold. Yet despite the passage of over 139 years since Claude Chana pulled the first gold nugget out of Auburn Ravine, the natural beauty of the Sierras, with their deep canyons and wooded mountainsides, remains as it must have looked when only the smoke from Indian campfires could be seen drifting through the clear mountain air.

As the first gold nuggets were pulled from miners' pans a short distance from the present location of Historic Auburn, changes began taking place which signaled the beginning of a new era. An area that had changed little for thousands of years was about to undergo a social revolution.

Gold lured thousands of men seeking great wealth into the foothills. Most of the miners had no intention of staying after they discovered enough gold to return home rich men. Along with the miners, however, came shopkeepers, craftsmen, and business leaders. These individuals became the pioneers of Placer County. They guided the area through its transitional years.

Prior to the discovery of gold and the successful crossing of the Sierras by the first wagon trains in the late 1840s, the area now known as Placer County was home to large numbers of Nisenan (often referred to as Southern Maidu) Indians.

Prior to May 16, 1848, when Chana discovered gold, only verbal history recorded the life-style of these people, who lived in the abundant foothills located between the high Sierras and the Sacramento Delta.

The first evidence of people living in the Auburn area was left by the Martis culture. The Martis later evolved into the Maidu Indians, whose culture was well-known in Northern California. The Martis apparently had a high-elevation hunting and seed-gathering culture. They mostly lived east of the main crest of the Sierras, but evidence has also placed them west of the ridge in the foothills and Auburn. The Martis inhabited the areas along the North and Middle forks of the American River. An arrowhead from the Martis culture was discovered near Auburn and has been identified as being from an era about 1,400 B.C. While the Martis were the first known group to inhabit the Auburn area, it was the Nisenan and Maidu Indians who had the greatest impact prior to the arrival of white settlers.

Unfortunately most California Indian cultures were unable to survive a series of plagues that greatly reduced their numbers when exposure to other cultures increased. Indian cultures which had lasted thousands of years were almost nonexistent 50 years after gold was discovered in California. It is estimated that 8,000 aborigines resided in the greater Placer County area in 1846. The number was cut in half by 1850, and census figures show only 900 Indians remained in the area by 1910.

For hundreds of years, however, the Nisenan occupied the areas along the Yuba, Bear, and American rivers as well as the lower drainage of the Feather River. Their territory extending from the crest of the Sierras to the banks of the Sacramento River, they thrived in the foothills. Natural grasses, oaks, pines, grassy meadows at higher elevations, and yearlong fresh mountain water supplied the Indians with those items necessary for survival.

The Nisenan recognized a number of political divisions within the tribe. Leadership was in the hands of a "headman," who was usually found in major population areas. The site of one of the largest populations was near the present-day intersection of the American and Sacramento rivers. Pusune, as it was known, was the primary center for political and cultural activity for the Nisenan.

Further east the Hill Nisenan could be found in smaller villages and groups ranging from single-family units to gatherings of 100 or more.

Throughout their history the Nisenan had little contact with areas outside the tribal territory. Only for purposes of trade, warfare, and ceremonial gatherings did the Nisenan leave the Auburn area. Because travel and communication were restricted to following the rivers leading from the mountains into the Sacramento Valley, the Valley Patwin, Nisenan, and Northern Maidu all shared similar cultural attitudes that led to cooperation for the good of all involved as well as for defense. Usually it was the men who traded with other villages and were aware of other tribes in the area. Women and children seldom left the territory.

Among the items traded by the Hill Nisenan to their valley counterparts were black oak acorns, pine nuts, manzanita berries, animal skins, and bow wood. In return Auburn area Nisenan received fish, roots, some types of grasses, shells, beads, salt, and feathers.

Village life consisted of a large center of activity with several smaller settlements nearby. At least 25 major villages were located along the American River from the confluence of the North and Middle forks to the Sacramento River. Those major villages located within five miles of present-day Auburn included Kotomyan, Hu'ul, Molman, Bisian, Siyakayan, and Chulku. Most of these villages contained a dance house, which gave them more importance in the eyes of the

An abundance of vegetation and a continuous supply of fresh water characterize the American River Valley, where the Nisenan Indians lived. Photo by John Elk III

Maidu Indians gathered in front of the last Indian Round-house in Auburn for this photo-graph in the 1930s. The Round-house, located near Indian Hills and Auburn Folsom roads, was used for tribal meetings and ceremonies. Courtesy, Berenice Pate

*Lizzi Enos, a Maidu Indian born in the 1880s, is pictured here with her granddaughter, Patsy Wren, in the early 1950s. Courtesy, **Auburn Journal***

Nisenan tribe. Some of these villages had as many as 500 people.

While the Nisenan were peaceful, arguments did occur over trespassing, hunting rights, and ceremonies. Often these disputes would lead to the departure of one family, which would leave to start a new village or move to a larger village. Tension outside each individual village was usually attributed to trespassing, social crimes, insults to leaders, or gambling. In the 1820s a series of confrontations between the hill and valley tribes resulted in the deaths of a number of Auburn and Nevada City Nisenan men in a battle near Roseville. The deaths provoked deep-seated hatred, and it was believed by many Nisenan that an epidemic in 1833 was caused by shamans sending bad air into the valley to avenge the killings. Hundreds of Valley Nisenan died during the epidemic.

Nisenan villages were built along low natural rises near streams and rivers. A village might have as many as 50 houses, each of which was 10 to 15 feet across, and covered with earth, tule mats, and grasses. Smaller houses were supported by upright poles and used during the warmer months for food gathering. The center

This snowscape in the Sierra Nevada Mountains gives an appreciation of the peace and beauty of the Placer County area prior to the discovery of gold and the influx of people. Photo by John Elk III

of social and political decision making was the village dance house. These semisubterranean structures had been sunk three or four feet into the ground. Held up by a series of large posts, they were covered by brush, which had a smoke hole in the top. Sweathouses were also constructed for treating the sick. While few Nisenan lived in caves, some evidence indicates they may have used caves as sweathouses.

Nisenan territory was well known to the men in the villages, and a series of trails connected key villages and rivers. The men's knowledge was put to use during food gathering and hunting activities, when different villages worked together. While the food could belong to individual families, the gathering and hunting pro-

vided an opportunity for different villages to acquire food for all members of the tribe. Acorns, sometimes ground into flour, were a staple food for the Nisenan. Roots were eaten raw, steamed, or made into cakes and stored for a winter food supply.

Berries, when in season, were used in a variety of ways, including use in a cider-like drink. In addition, they were traded to Valley Nisenan.

Hunting was usually a joint effort between villages. The best marksmen from each village would join together for the kill after other hunters encircled the herd and drove it into the center where the marksmen were placed.

A great deal of Nisenan ceremony surrounded a bear hunt. Even though black bears were hunted in the winter months, the California grizzlies were feared and, more often than not, left alone by the hunting parties. Wildcats and mountain lions, on the other hand, were used for both food and clothing.

The Nisenan also perfected snares and traps for capturing rabbits and other small animals. Rivers in the area provided fishing opportunities. Some Nisenan used nets and harpoons thrown from log canoes, but most of the time the fish were driven into shallow areas of the river and caught by hand.

When trading parties returned from the valley, they often brought salmon and sturgeon from the Sacramento River back into the foothills. Salt was obtained in the Lincoln and Cool areas and added to the Nisenan diet.

Above, left: This blind Digger Indian woman, photographed in October 1912, lived to be over 108 years old. Courtesy, Berenice Pate

Left: A number of Auburn residents dressed in Indian clothing and joined other area Indians for this early 1920s photo for the Auburn Gold Show. Among those photographed were Henry Gietzen and John Robinson. Courtesy, Berenice Pate

Orchards and vineyards grace the foothills of Placer County with beauty, at the same time representing a profitable income. Courtesy, Placer County Chamber of Commerce

Nisenan clothing was based on the time of year. During the summer months men often went naked or wore a breechcloth of deerskin. Women wore short aprons made of wire grass, shredded maple, or willow bark. During colder weather the Auburn area Nisenan used fur blankets and skins. Some rabbit robes were made of as many as 40 skins, which were cut into strips and woven into garments.

Grooming included long hair and even beards for the men. Sharp stones and burning embers were used to cut hair. Whiskers were pulled with the help of shells.

The family structure provided a great deal of support in the villages. Older women assisted younger village women with childbirth. Once a baby was born the Nisenan waited 16 days before displaying the infant to relatives and others. Before marriage the man asked the woman for her permission. If she agreed to the marriage, he then asked her parents. In some Nisenan villages the man moved in with his future wife and her family, and assisted with hunting and fishing for six months. Then the couple returned to the man's parents, a separate bed was made, and they were considered married.

Decisions regarding tribal law and life were made by a headman. Since he had little real authority, he generally served as an advisor. He often named his successor, and, if no competent male relative could be found, a female could succeed him as advisor. The headman also served at ceremonial gatherings and assisted with the distribution of food.

Because the Sierras represented an impregnable wall along the eastern edge of the Nisenan territory, they remained out of reach of what was taking place in other sections of California.

The Spanish who arrived in California never reached the foothills. Jose Canizares came close to

Nisenan territory in 1776, but he stopped southwest of the Miwok areas of the state. Spanish explorers transported many Miwok Indians to the California missions, but no records of Nisenan involvement can be found.

During 1808 Spanish explorer Gabriel Moraga was one of the first non-natives to cross Nisenan territory. In 1813 the systematic transportation of Indians to the missions led to a battle between the forces of Spanish military leader Luis A. Arguello and the Miwok near the mouth of the Cosumnes River.

As more and more Indians were transported, the Nisenan did allow Miwok Indians escaping from the missions into their territory. The Nisenan themselves continued to be left alone and to enjoy the peaceful life-style to which they had become accustomed over hundreds of years.

Even during the 1820s, as trappers from the American and Hudson's Bay Company began to settle along the American River and the higher elevations of the Sierras, the trappers and the Indians coexisted peacefully. It seemed that the foothills not only provided the Hill Nisenan with all of the items they needed for survival but protected them from outside influences as well.

Right: One of the first explorers of the West, John C. Frémont, twice crossed the Sierra Nevadas in winter and later campaigned for the Bear Flag Revolt and other subsequent wars. Courtesy, The Bancroft Library, University of California, Berkeley

Above, right: John Sutter, American pioneer of the West, established his fort in Northern California where it became a trade center and rendezvous for newcomers coming through the Sierra Nevadas. Sutter was known as a trapper, farmer, merchant, and military ruler. However, when gold was discovered at his sawmill in 1848, squatters overtook his land and he lost his fortune in the gold rush that followed. Courtesy, Cirker's Dictionary of American Portraits

When the epidemic of 1833 struck the Valley Nisenan, the Auburn area tribes suffered little. Believed to be malaria the epidemic swept through the Sacramento Valley, wiping out entire villages. Surviving Valley Nisenan moved to the foothills in an effort to avoid the sickness. Some experts say 75 percent of the Valley Nisenan population fell victim to the epidemic.

Captain John Sutter, who settled in Nisenan territory in 1839, encountered little opposition from the Indians. Many of the Miwoks moved from their villages on the Cosumnes River to live near Sutter's Fort. Most of the Valley Nisenan also remained in the area on peaceful terms with the growing number of settlers. Sharing their knowledge with their new white neighbors, the Nisenan and Miwok Indians had little to fear.

One of the first white explorers to enter the area was Captain John C. Fremont. Along with Kit Carson, Fremont and his group crossed the Sierras during the spring of 1844. Fighting heavy snows, they battled their way through the natural elements and arrived at the headwaters of the South Fork of the American River. Eventually the group camped near Coloma, then followed the South Fork to the intersection of the Middle and North forks of the American. From there they continued along the river to reach Sutter's Fort, where they were warmly received by Sutter.

Fremont and Sutter had a great deal in common, including their love for the Sierras and the surrounding foothills. Fremont's crossing of the Sierras signaled the beginning of a new overland migration into California. Fremont's explorers paid a heavy price for the winter crossing of the Sierras. They had no wagons, but began the trip with 67 horses and mules. When they reached Sutter's Fort, only 33 of the animals remained. Many fell into the deep canyons as the group worked its way down the western slopes of the mountains. Loss of the animals was devastating for Fremont and his party, but he was grateful he and his men had survived the winter crossing.

As Fremont and his men enjoyed the comforts of Sutter's Fort, the first group to make the crossing in wagons was just leaving Council Bluffs, Iowa, and heading for the California Emigrant's Trail. Elisha Stevens, captain of the Stevens-Townsend-Murphy Party, headed west with 23 men, 8 women (of whom 2 were pregnant), 15 children, and 11 wagons. Stevens, a former trapper and blacksmith, was elected wagonmaster, and Caleb Greenwood, an old mountain man, was hired as guide. Greenwood was accompanied by his two sons, the offspring from his relationship with a Crow Indian squaw. Among those who took part in the journey was Dr. John Townsend. As the group traveled west to the Humboldt Sink, where the river gradually disappeared into the ground about 80 miles east of Reno, it had plenty of provisions but little idea of which way to proceed.

Greenwood's contract had run out, and he had little knowledge of the area past the Rocky Mountains. Finding an old Indian who knew the area ahead, Greenwood used dirt drawings and sign language to learn that a river about 50 miles west of the group's location would provide them with a trail west.

The Indian, a chief named Truckee, agreed to guide the Stevens Party. Dr. Townsend, Stevens, and Joseph Foster started out to explore the trail. Three days later they returned to the wagon train after finding the river described by Truckee. Reaching what is now the Truckee River near Wadsworth, Nevada, the Stevens Party began the journey up the river into the Sierras near the present border between California and Nevada. With snow already falling the group reached the present location of the town of Truckee on November 14. Since there was no direct path to follow, a small group was sent south toward Lake Tahoe in hopes of finding a trail. The rest of the party with the wagons continued along a tributary (now Donner Creek) and reached Donner Lake.

With two feet of snow on the ground, the Stevens Party continued west along a trail close to the path later used by the Central Pacific to cross over the Sierras. After crossing the summit on November 25, the group continued on to the present location of Big Bend,

Orchards of peaches, pears, plums, berries, figs, and oranges spread over the foothills of Placer County. Courtesy, Placer County Chamber of Commerce

where snow forced them to stop. A cabin was built for protection against the winter snows, and the women and children were left behind while the men continued on to Sutter's Fort for help. When they arrived at Sutter's Fort, they were joined by the smaller group that had left on horseback near Donner Lake to look for a southern passage over the Sierras.

With their families still in the mountains, the men of the Stevens Party were either forced to fight by the Mexican governor of California or volunteered to take part in the revolution occurring in the state. Stevens' men traveled as far south as Santa Barbara during the revolution before they were able to return to Sutter's Fort and the Sierras to bring their families the rest of the distance. It wasn't until February 1845 that they were able to rejoin their families and bring them to safety.

The Stevens Party was the first group to make it across the Sierras by following the Truckee Route, but it certainly wasn't the best known. It was the tragedy of the Donner Party that remains a symbol of the difficulties early settlers faced in making the mountain crossing.

Arriving at the foot of the range in October 1846, George and Jacob Donner led a group of 86 people into the mountains, where they were stopped by heavy snow. Only half of the members of the Donner Party survived the winter. Four relief parties traveled from Sutter's Fort to rescue those people who were still alive.

After the successful crossing by the Stevens Party in 1844, 50 wagons made the crossing in 1845 and another 500 in 1846. The first year after gold was discovered, thousands of wagons crossed the Sierras. Many of them traveled through Placer County close to the present-day location of Interstate 80. By 1848 two easier crossings had been discovered: the Carson Pass and the Lassen Route. Soon most of the wagon trains were taking other routes across the Sierras, and avoiding some of the hardships experienced by earlier travelers.

Ironically, Claude Chana, the man who later became the first to discover gold in Auburn Ravine, was for a short time a member of the Donner Party. Chana, traveling with the California Company, caught up to the Donner Party and traveled with them for a short time. Because the Donner Party seemed to be traveling slowly, Chana and the California Company went on ahead. Two years later Chana joined three other Frenchmen, one of whom had been with Fremont on his journey, and 25 Nisenan Indians to form a party for a trip to Coloma. Instead of traveling back to Sutter's Fort, the group chose a course straight across the foothills from Theodore Sigard's ranch to the location of John Marshall's gold discovery. The second night out Chana and the others camped along Auburn Ravine. The next day he discovered gold near the present location of Historic Auburn. The date was May 16, 1848.

Facing page: At one time Placer
County held the record of being
the largest single shipping point
in the United States for fresh
fruit. Pictured here are fruit
pickers at one of the many
groves in the area. Courtesy,
Placer County Chamber of
Commerce

Left: These miners stand next to
a hydraulic pump, a more
sophisticated method of mining
than panning in a river.

Below: Believed to be one of the
first photographic records of
Auburn Ravine miners, this
photo was taken in 1852 near
the present location of Historic
Auburn. Courtesy, Jim Johnson

Chapter
II

Gold
Brings
Changes

1849-1861

Camping along the bank of Auburn Ravine Creek the second night out on his trip to Coloma, Claude Chana rose with the sun in hopes of trying his newfound skills as a gold miner. The rest of the members of Chana's party were beginning to pack the horses and break camp to resume the journey. Everyone was in a hurry to get to the site where gold had been found some 20 miles away. But when Chana dipped his gold pan into the cold rushing water, he made a discovery that would lead to the forming of a new city, provide untold fortunes for some, and spell disaster for others: Gold!

As the sand washed away, Chana glanced at the edge of his pan and found three good-sized gold nuggets. The other members of the group were as quick to join him at the edge of the creek as they had been to prepare to leave. For the remainder of May 1848, the group continued to pan for gold along Auburn Ravine and into Baltimore Ravine, just south of present-day Auburn.

Word of Chana's discovery traveled farther downstream along the American River to Sinclair's Ranch. Sinclair immediately gathered a group of Indians and traveled to the Auburn area. Feeling that the gold along the American was of a better quality, Sinclair attempted to convince Chana to join him on the American. Chana, however, elected to stay along the Auburn Ravine.

Inexperience on the part of the new miners, as well as high expectations and word that a larger discovery had been unearthed on the Yuba River, resulted in the splitting up of Chana's party. The party had only three pounds of gold to show for three weeks of work. Discouraged, part of the group continued on to Coloma, while Chana moved on to the Yuba River discovery. Chana spent only three weeks along the Auburn Ravine after he discovered gold. He would never return to mine Auburn Ravine Creek. To the man who first discovered gold in Auburn, the fortunes of the gold fields brought only brief prosperity. Chana did have good luck along the Yuba River, however, and in October 1849 he returned to his friend Sigard's ranch on the Bear River. For the sum of $6,000 (gold was selling for $16 an ounce in 1849), he purchased his old friend's ranch.

Chana's fortunes were about to turn in 1850, when California was brought into the Union. Sigard had obtained his land from a land grant, and Chana discovered that the title was not clear. After a series of legal battles, he held title to only 500 acres. What wasn't taken away by the courts, Chana lost to the floods of 1861-62. Mud from hydraulic mines upstream washed over his agricultural lands, leaving nothing usable behind. What he had purchased for $6,000 in 1848, Chana sold for $500 14 years later. Broke, he moved to

*A horsedrawn wagon pulls an
iron bridge section along the
Foresthill Road. Freight delivery in Placer County depended
upon horse and ox trains. Courtesy,* **Auburn Journal**

Wheatland and spent his remaining years making
grape wine and collecting a toll on his road and bridge
over the Bear River. Chana died on May 24, 1882, and
was buried in Wheatland.

While Chana's fortune slipped through his hands,
others replaced him along Auburn Ravine Creek.
Nicholas Algier soon arrived at that location. Algier
reportedly was the first miner to take large amounts of
gold out of Auburn Ravine. As word spread, however,
Algier was joined by many other miners. The area
called North Fork Dry Diggings soon was a hotbed of
activity.

Samuel Seabough, an early Placer County historian, wrote of the area: "In the Dry Diggings, near
Auburn, during the month of August 1848, one man
got $16,000 out of five cart-loads of dirt. In the same
diggings a good many were collecting from $800 to
$1,500 a day."

The following summer the tent city that was home
for the miners gave way to the first wood and fabric

buildings. Stores handling supplies for miners and
catering to the needs of the fortune seekers formed the
basis for the future city of Auburn.

During the winter of 1849 heavy snows and rain
slowed the migration of miners into the Sierras. Many
miners spent the winter in the newly-formed community of Auburn, which may have been named by Dr. Di-
mon after his hometown of Auburn, New York. Trying
to stay warm and dry, the miners lived in shacks built of
wood and canvas. Gold prices and difficult access into
the area drove commodity prices up. A bottle of gin
went for $6, sugar was $1 a pound, and a pair of pants
could cost as much as $23. Gold, not cash, was the ac-
cepted form of payment during the winter of 1849 to

1850. What cost $247 in 1848 was available for $33.50 in 1881.

Early miners in Auburn came in all shapes and sizes and from all educational backgrounds and social strata. Not all the miners were cut from the rugged cloth often associated with gold miners. On some days, eyewitnesses reported, you could see miners in high hats, white shirts, and gloves.

One common aspect of mining life was that it was a male society. The first two women didn't arrive in Auburn until late in 1849, and population figures for the town in 1850 show there were 1,265 males and 23 females. When Placer County was formed census figures listed 345 females in the county.

Eliza Elliott Gibson is recognized as the second white woman to reside in Auburn. (Mrs. H.J. Crandall, described in Chapter VI, was the first). Arriving in the spring of 1850, she remained in the city until 1864, when she moved to Nevada. Gibson was described by

Below: After gold was discovered along Auburn Ravine in 1848, most miners found that the American River, below Auburn, was a better mining location. Dozens of mining camps thus sprang up along the river. Courtesy, **Auburn Journal**

Right: These gold miners take a break to pose for this 1860s picture. Courtesy, **Auburn Journal**

Above: Maine Bar in Placer County was a mining town during the Gold Rush era. Courtesy, Auburn Journal

Left: Mining was a profitable industry throughout Placer County. Courtesy, Placer County Chamber of Commerce

Seen here are miners panning
for gold along the American
River in Placer County. Courtesy, **Auburn Journal**

Auburn residents as a "kind-hearted, capable, and industrious business lady." Remembered by many as the "good Samaritan" of Auburn, she died in her home in Silver City, Nevada, on March 11, 1872.

While the early miners sought gold, other settlers were fanning the winds of political change in the state and the county. With the formation of California in 1850, Auburn became part of Yuba County.

It wasn't until April 28, 1851, that a legislative act created Placer County, and made Auburn its county seat. Douglas Fry, Joseph Walkup, William Gwynn, H.M. House, and Jonathan Roberts were chosen to serve on a Board of Commissioners, which was responsible for establishing election precincts and receiving and counting votes. The first county election was held on May 26, 1851.

Voters selected County Judge Hugh Fitzsimmons, District Attorney R.D. Hopkins, County Clerk James T. Stewart, Sheriff Samuel C. Austin, County Surveyor

Samuel B. Wyman, County Assessor Alfred Lewis, County Treasurer Douglas Bingham, and County Coroner John C. Montgomery. The total number of votes cast in the first election was 2,792.

Even with the arrival of organized government, Auburn remained a frontier town. Those arriving in Auburn and Placer County did so on foot or horseback. It wasn't until 1850 that William Gregory formed the first stage route to Auburn. A year later as many as six stages, pulled by four to six horses, arrived daily.

Freight arrived by oxcart from Sacramento. The two-day trip covered 45 miles, and each wagon could haul 9,500 pounds of goods. Later the slower oxcarts

*These lumbermen take a break
to pose for this photo. Courtesy,*
Auburn Journal

were replaced by pack trains of 40 to 50 mules. Each mule could carry up to 500 pounds.

Commerce developed almost as fast as the miners arrived. In the middle of the summer of 1849, William Gwynn and H.M. House opened a store in Auburn. A short time later Captain John A. Sutter also established a trading post for miners in the area. Composed mostly of tents, the business district didn't begin to take shape until three years later, when wooden buildings replaced the tents. Even then commerce remained tied to the locations of the miners. As the miners moved so did the stores and trading posts. When Auburn became the Placer County seat, business became much more stable.

The new stage routes also provided transport from the foothills to San Francisco bank vaults for the gold. Gold not only provided great personal wealth, but it also gave rise to a number of new businesses.

Known as the crossroads of the mother lode, Auburn soon became a financial center as well. Gregory's Express was the first express company to open its doors in Auburn in 1849, purchasing gold dust from miners. Adams & Co. arrived in November of the

same year. Within months of opening its doors in San Francisco in 1852, Wells, Fargo and Co. opened an office in Auburn under the direction of John Q. Jackson. For Jackson, Auburn provided an opportunity much to his liking.

In a letter to his brother on October 23, 1852, Jackson wrote of his Auburn experiences:

This is a responsible position and one, by which, in my good management of business conduct, I have gained the utmost confidence of the heads of concerns in San Francisco and Sacramento. What I have to do is quite confining—staying in my office all day until 10 at night buying dust, forwarding and receiving packages of every kind, from and to everywhere—filling out drafts for the eastern mails in all sorts of sums …the gold dust bought during the last two days is to be cleaned, weighed, sealed, and packed ready to be forwarded in the morning.

Two years later Jackson again described Auburn life in a letter to his brother:

Auburn as it is situated is the place of the most business of the county …the amount of gold dust bought and sold at the Yankee Jims, Iowa Hill, and Michigan Bluff, *in the aggregate, is from $80,000 to $100,000 per month. At this office from $30,000 to $50,000 and at Rattlesnake Bar office from $30,000 to $40,000 ...when we make a shipment 'tis frequently 100 to 150 pounds, about as much as one likes to shoulder to and from the stages. The mining in the rivers is in full blast and some claims paying remarkably well. I go to a place called Murderers Bar, six miles distant, once a week to purchase dust dug there. I hear a great deal of complaint among the miners—many are doing nothing. While one man is making $10 or $20 per day there are dozens who are scarcely making board.*

Next to gold the most desired commodity was news from other sections of the country. Mail service was established with some degree of regularity in March 1851. Of the 60 post offices in the state that year, 26 were in foothill mining towns. Four years later Placer

*The Freeman Hotel, like other hotels in the area, had taxi wagons that took visitors to and from the Placer County Courthouse daily. The Freeman was a popular meeting place for both social and political events. Courtesy, **Auburn Journal***

County had 12 post offices. Residents often had to wait months for news from home as mail from the eastern states was transported by ship around the Horn or through the Isthmus of Panama. Auburn's first post office opened its doors on July 21, 1853, with J.F. Baily as postmaster.

Increases in population also brought schools and churches to Auburn. Public education did not yet exist, and schools were privately operated. Each had one room, and all grades attended at the same time. Every week parents would pay a tuition fee to keep a particular school in business. One of the first, operated by a Mrs. Horton, was situated near the present location of the Shanghai Restaurant. Another school soon opened in the Methodist Church at the intersection of High and Sacramento streets. (The Methodist Church later burned down.)

By 1856 county records show Placer County had 628 children between 4 and 18 years of age. Auburn was the center of population with 127 school-age children. Iowa Hill had 90 students, and Illinoistown had another 85. In 1849 California's Constitution had provided for a school system, but it wasn't until 1855 that Placer County elected H.E. Force as superintendent of schools.

*Above: Students line up outside
Auburn Grammar School in the
late 1890s. Located on Railroad
Street, the upper floors were
added to the buildings in 1872.
The buildings contained one
grammar, one intermediate,
and two primary classrooms.
Courtesy,* Auburn Journal

*Left: A Birdsall Olive Oil wagon
sits in front of the Auburn Volunteer Fire Department Station
in East Auburn in the early
1890s. Courtesy,* Auburn
Journal

One of the biggest threats faced by residents in Auburn during the 1850s and 1860s was fire. Due to the long dry summers, the wood and cloth construction of many of the structures, and a lack of water, fire often could destroy towns within minutes.

The first big fire in a Placer County community was reported in Ophir on July 12, 1853. Starting with the Union Hotel the fire burned the entire downtown area. When it was out only two buildings remained standing on Main Street. An estimated 60 buildings burned at a loss of $90,000. Two years later on June 4, 1855, a fire started in a house located below the Methodist Church in Auburn. Flames traveled up the hill and crossed the street, burning Dr. Rinzie's drugstore. Soon Diana Bowling Saloon, Keehner's Bakery, George H. Stephens' Livery Stable, and the Empire and Orleans hotels were in flames. Everyone able to help worked to carry items out of the buildings to the nearby hills for safety. The fire only lasted 1 hour and 20 minutes, but it burned 80 buildings to the ground. Officials valued the loss of structures at $215,000.

Fighting fires in the early days was a difficult task since there was little water and even less fire fighting equipment. At first fire fighting consisted simply of a bucket brigade that was formed when the fire began. Meeting in the courthouse the first Auburn Hook and Ladder Company was formed on November 8, 1852. Charles McKee was elected foreman, Isaac W. Credit was first assistant, and John Bazley was second assistant. Fund-raising was started to purchase hook and ladders, and the first collection amounted to $70.

By the summer of 1853, 14 volunteers made up the fire fighting force. Meeting the first and third Tuesdays of each month, the Hook and Ladder Company began to build a responsive fire fighting company. After the 1855 fire Auburn public buildings and places of business were ordered to keep water barrels to help fight fires. P.C. Rust, H.M. House, and a Mr. Johnson were named Auburn fire wardens.

In addition several of the buildings that replaced those which had burned were designed to be fireproof. A three-story brick wall was built next to the American Hotel to help stop the spread of future fires. After a fire in 1857 the Auburn Water Works (Smith & Wooden) put in a 2,000-foot iron pipe at a cost of $1,560 to help bring water into the downtown area to

Members of the East Auburn Volunteer Fire Department check out water pressure in front of Firehouse No. 1, built in 1888. The firehouse was later moved to its present location on Lincoln Way near the Auburn Railroad Depot. Courtesy, Jim Johnson

The North Saloon was a common watering-hole for lumbermen and miners. Courtesy, **Auburn Journal**

fight fires. Despite these increased efforts, many fires continued to destroy individual buildings. For years volunteers had to rely on buckets and a two-wheeled hand cart to fight fires.

Fire may have been the most difficult problem faced by a growing community, but crime was also on the increase with so much gold being transported from Auburn to San Francisco. Immediately after Chana's discovery little thought was given to crime. It simply did not exist. Crime, when it did occur, met with a swift and often terrible response. In the absence of courts, punishment was usually handled with a rope and a tree. Often even suspicion brought punishment. Suspects had to prove their innocence or suffer the consequences. Those members of the community who did not have a job or appeared to be unknown to area residents were more often than not told to leave town.

The first major crime occurred late in 1848 along the trail leading from Auburn to the American River crossing. Some miners were bringing gold dust out of the canyon on horseback when they were robbed. As

they approached a grove of trees, a shot was fired from the direction of the trees, and the lead rider fell to the ground. Four or five Mexicans came from the trees, captured the horse carrying the gold, and left toward Sutter's Fort. By the time the other members of the group realized what had happened, the outlaws had gotten away. An effort was made to go after them, but no one was ever caught in the first Placer County highway robbery.

On October 20, 1853, a murder was committed near Traveler's Rest in Auburn. Andrew King and Robert Scott got into an argument after King refused to lend Scott three dollars at a gambling table. The next day Scott called King out, demanding that King take a weapon and defend himself. As King turned to enter the house, Scott drew his revolver and killed him. Scott was traced to the Cosumnes River, where he was arrested by Constable M.P.H. Love and Deputy Sheriff E.B. Boust. Scott was tried and found guilty. On February 13, 1854, Judge Howell ordered the execution of Scott, which occurred on March 31 of the same year.

Built in 1866, the Freeman Hotel was a popular resting stop for people traveling to Placer County to do business at the Placer County Courthouse. The hotel was conveniently located across the street from the Auburn train depot. Courtesy, **Auburn Journal**

The execution attracted the attention of a number of Auburn townspeople; in fact, 2,000 people were in town for the hanging. While members of the Hook and Ladder Company served as guards, Scott was brought to the gallows. According to the *Placer Herald*, the day went as follows:

At the hour of half-past eleven a.m., he was released from his irons and dressed in a becoming manner. With his hands tied behind him, he was taken in a wagon from the jail to the place of execution, followed by a large crowd of people. During his course to the gallows, Scott appeared perfectly cool and unmoved. Upon arrival at the gallows, the prisoner mounted the stairs with a quick and firm step. The crowd around the gallows was now very dense. The sheriff read the order of the court.

Scott was given a chance to address the crowd. Stepping forward, he spoke his last words:

I have but few words to say. I have had a fair and impartial trial, and am willing to abide by the law. I have one no more than I would do again to any man who would not give me satisfaction for what he had said. As for the paltry mob who have urged on my trial before I was ready, they are too mean for my curses.

The *Herald* article went on to say:

The prisoner was dressed in a white robe. A black cap was drawn over his head, his feet securely tied, and placed in his proper position upon the trap, with the rope around his neck. The sheriff announced the hour to be 12 o'clock, when the lever which worked the machinery was pushed forward, the trap fell, and Robert Scott's spirit was ushered into the presence of his God.

While Scott was the first man sentenced to hang by a Placer County court, he certainly wasn't the last. Death

Facing page: While the new Placer County Courthouse stands in the background, the old wooden Placer County Courthouse is seen in the foreground. The older building was removed shortly after the new courthouse was put into use. Courtesy, Auburn Journal

This Central Pacific Railroad timetable in 1865 shows daily train service between Auburn and Sacramento. Courtesy, Auburn Journal

CENTRAL PACIFIC RAILROAD
OF CALIFORNIA.

LELAND STANFORD, President.
C. P. HUNTINGTON, Vice-President.
MARK HOPKINS, Treasurer.
E. B. CROCKER, Att'y and Gen'l Agent.
E. H. MILLER, JR, Secretary.
W. H. PORTER, Cashier.
S. S. MONTAGUE, Chief Engineer.
B. B. REDDING, Land Commissioner.

Principal Offices,
SACRAMENTO, CAL.,
AND
54 William Street,
NEW YORK CITY.

CHAS. CROCKER, General Superintendent.
JNO. CORNING, Ass't Gen'l Superintendent.
E. C. FELLOWS, Sup't Sacramento Division.
F. W. BOWEN, Sup't Truckee Division.
C. E. GILLETT, Sup't Shoshone and Humboldt Div'ns.
JAS. CAMPBELL, Sup't Salt Lake Div'n.
E. F. PERKINS, Sup't M. Power and M.
T. H. GOODMAN, Gen'l Frey'r. and Pass'gr Ag't.

Leave Sacramento			Dist's	THROUGH TIME TABLE, May 17, 1869.	Elev'n	Arrive at Sacramento.		
Mixed	Acc'm	Expr's				Expr's	Acc'm	Mixed
A.M.	P.M.	A.M.	Miles	**SACRAMENTO DIVISION.**	Feet	P.M.	A.M.	P.M.
5.00	2.00	6.30	0	Sacramento	56	1.20	10.00	6.30
		*7.40	18	Junction	189	*12.30		
		7.55	22	Rocklin	269	12.00		
		8.40	36	Auburn	1,385	11.00		
12.40	7.30	9.50	54	Colfax	2,448	9.50	12.00	12.40
		10.25	64	Gold Run	3,245	8.46		
		10.33	67	Dutch Flat	3,425	8.32		
5.20	12.10	*12.15	92	Cisco	5,911	*6.20	8 10	7.55
P.M.	A.M.	A.M.	105	Summit	7,042	5.05	P.M.	A.M.
9.00	5.30	2.10	120	Truckee	5,866	4.20	5.00	5.00
		2.35	128	Boca	5,560	3.42		
		4.20	154	Reno	4,525	2.10		
		5.25	174	Clarks	4,290	12.50		
A.M.	P.M.	P.M.		**TRUCKEE DIVISION.**		A.M.	A.M.	P.M.
7.00	2.45	*6.30	189	Wadsworth	4,104	12.05	8.00	9.00
		8.26	223	White Plains	3,921	9.43		
		9 05	235	Brown's	3,955	9.05		
		10.25	262	Oreana	4,206	7.45		
		11 25	284	Humboldt	4,262	*6.40		
		12.00	296	Mill City	4,256	5.36		
		1.00	313	Rose Creek	4,348	4.45		
P.M.	A.M.	A.M.		**SHOSHONE DIVISION.**		P.M.	P.M.	A.M.
8.00	6.10	1.45	324	Winnemucca	4,355	4.10	3.45	7.50
		2.35	341	Golconda	4,419	3.15		
		3.50	365	Stone House	4,449	2.00		
		4.30	379	Battle Mountain	4,534	1.15		
		5.25	396	Argenta	4,575	12.25		
		6.00	407	Shoshone	4,665	11.30		
		6.30	417	Be-o-wa-we	4,717	11.05		
		7.25	435	Palisade	4,870	10.15		
A.M.	P.M.	A.M.		**HUMBOLDT DIVISION.**		A.M.	A.M.	P.M.
10.30	7.15	8.30	445	Carlin	4,930	9.35	4.00	8.00
		*10.00	468	Elko	5,030	*8.25		
		10.30	478	Osino	5,100			
		11.05	488	Peko	5,220			
		12.30	517	Tulasco	5,418			
		12.55	525	Wells	5,650			
		1.45	539	Independence	6,115			
		2.25	551	Pequop	6,180			
P.M.	A.M.	P.M.		**SALT LAKE DIVISION.**		P.M.	P.M.	A.M.
11.40	7 30	*3 15	559	Toano	5,964	11.00	4.45	9.30
			577	Montello	4,800			
			609	Bovine	4,253			
			621	Terrace	4,450			
			636	Matlin	4,821			
			669	Monument	4,290			
10.50	8.00	9 55	690	Terminus	4,943	1.00	3.55	9.40
A.M.	P.M.	A.M.		**U.P.R.R.**		P.M.	A.M.	P.M.
Arrive at Terminus.			742	Ogden	4,320	Leave Terminus.		
		A.M. 9.30	1774	Omaha	965	4.20 P.M.		

Express Trains run "Daily." *Meals

by hanging was almost certain punishment for anyone found guilty of murder during the first 20 years after Placer County was formed.

News from other parts of the state and the nation was a major topic in every section of the new county, but news often took months to get to the foothills. While some eastern newspapers found their way into Placer County, the demand for a county paper produced the *Placer Herald*. Founded on September 11, 1852, the *Placer Herald* was the first newspaper in Placer County. Since that time it has not missed a week of publication under the same banner. First published by Tabb Mitchell, Richard Durst, and John McElroy, the *Placer Herald* proclaimed itself to be a newspaper with little interest in politics aside from "equal and exact justice for all."

History has shown, however, that the *Placer Herald* became a voice for the Democratic viewpoint in Placer County. As a result a number of Republican papers were later formed to counter that viewpoint. One of the first major efforts on the part of the *Placer Herald* was active support for the incorporation of Auburn. Strong editorial support began in 1855 and continued for the next five years in an effort to form the new city within Placer County. After a long and often heated exchange of viewpoints, the city was incorporated by a legislative act on March 29, 1861.

One and one-quarter miles square with a courthouse in the center of town, Auburn soon found itself in the middle of another controversy. Recognizing the importance of bringing a railroad to Auburn from Sacramento, the town voted a subsidy of $50,000 on June 4, 1860, to help build the Sacramento, Placer and Nevada Railroad. It came within five miles of Auburn before construction stopped. A stage line completed the distance between Auburn Station, as it was known, and the city of Auburn.

Hopes for completion fell as the Central Pacific began construction of the transcontinental railroad over the Sierras. As the Central Pacific's drive east brought it closer to Auburn, it was obvious the Sac-

ramento, Placer, and Nevada Railroad would not be finished. Fearing it would have to pay off the $50,000 debt against the railroad, Auburn's city fathers had the act of incorporation repealed on March 30, 1868. From that time until May 2, 1888, Auburn had no city government and got along the best it could.

Building a railroad across the Sierras had been a dream ever since the first pioneers crossed the mountains. It wasn't until June 28, 1861, that the Central Pacific Railroad Company of California was incorporated in Sacramento. Eight years later the link connecting east and west was made with the Union

Wood is stacked along the Central Pacific Railroad track in 1868 during the construction of the railroad through Placer County. Early trains were all wood burning steam engines. Most of the trees along the track were cut in order to keep the trains running. Courtesy,
Auburn Journal

Pacific at Promontory Point, Utah. To get the project underway President Abraham Lincoln signed the Pacific Railroad Bill into law in 1862. The bill provided the necessary financial assistance to build the railroad. The Central Pacific was in the hands of Leland Stanford, a grocer; Charles Crocker, a dry goods merchant; and Collis P. Huntington and his partner Mark Hopkins, both in the hardware business. While the financial end of the railroad was in the hands of these men, who became known as the "Big Four," the actual building of the railroad was up to engineer Theodore Judah.

At the point when the Central Pacific reached Newcastle in June 1864, the Big Four had invested all of their own money to take it that far. It took a series of congressional acts to keep it going. One provided for cash bonuses of $16,000 per mile of construction on level ground and $48,000 per mile in mountain territory. While Judah and his survey crew were high in the Sierras, the Central Pacific owners were in Washington, D.C., on an important mission. A California Supreme Court ruling said that the Sierras started at a point 31 miles east of Sacramento. The Big Four, however, man-

aged to get President Lincoln to move the line to 24 miles east of Sacramento. The change added another $700,000 to the Central Pacific treasury for the track already in place to Newcastle.

Trains began to run regularly from Sacramento to Newcastle, bringing curious travelers from the state capital. Newcastle at one point was described by a traveler as a "dismal place with two saloons for every shop." But excursionists found the Placer County community pleasant and often took the train for a day's outing in the country.

Lacking popular support in both San Francisco financial circles and Placer County politics, the Central Pacific continued working its way east. At one point the railroad was accused by the *Placer Herald* and county supervisors of planning the "Dutch Flat Swindle." Some people felt the railroad could never be built over the Sierras and that it would instead go only as far as Dutch Flat. From that point many felt the Big Four would control a large operation transporting freight over the Sierras to the Comstock Lode in Nevada. This scheme was believed to be the real reason for building

Used to help construct the railroad bridge that now crosses Interstate 80, this railroad was built down Sacramento Street, between the east- and west-bound tracks. Railroad crews would pick up one section of track from the rear of the train and lay it in front of the engine. The rails never ran the complete distance between the east- and west-bound tracks. Courtesy, The Mel Locher Collection

the railroad. Supporters of the theory pointed to the fact that no railroad had ever been built over such a mountain range in either Europe or the United States. Expectations that the railroad would cross the Sierras through Placer County met with a great deal of resistance.

Although the railroad appeared to be based on solid engineering plans, attracting people to build it was difficult. The pay of five dollars a day was considered a good wage, but most railroad workers couldn't resist the attraction of the gold and silver fields in Nevada.

Crocker came forward with the idea of using Chinese laborers. Soon the Chinese were out working in full force on the railroad. Earning only two dollars a day they reportedly did twice the work of the Irish laborers who had built the railroad as far as Newcastle. The Chinese were also willing to be suspended in baskets to chip away at the ledge east of Colfax and around Cape Horn, above the American River.

By May 1866 Central Pacific construction crews made up of 7,500 Chinese, 2,500 Caucasians, and 600

teams of horses had worked their way 10 miles past Dutch Flat. When they were stalled by the snows of the winter of 1866-1867, Crocker decided to build huge sleds to carry equipment to the lower elevation construction locations. Central Pacific crews worked their way down the eastern slopes to Truckee and on to the connection with the Union Pacific.

Like the discovery of gold 20 years earlier, the construction of the railroad over the Sierras would have dramatic effects on Placer County in the years to come.

Chapter III

Auburn
Comes
of Age

1862-1916

Early pioneers of Placer County had little desire to duplicate the comforts of the homes they had left in the East. Life was not easy in the foothills, and for every ounce of gold taken from the rivers and streams of the Sierras, the early miners were that much closer to returning to their homes and friends in the East.

After nearly 25 years of growth, however, a new era began in Placer County—an era of people putting down roots. Farms began producing cash crops because the railroad provided a means for getting products to market. Hydraulic mining was entering its most productive period. The Placer County government was strong and had plenty of cash reserves. After a decade of fighting, lawsuits, and disagreements between the county and the Central Pacific Railroad, Placer County was prepared to sell its 2,500 shares of railroad stock. The year was 1870.

Agriculture was still in its infancy in the foothills, and most area residents turned to mining for their economic base. Technology had provided miners with an alternative to placer and hard rock mining. With the help of the American River, which flowed down from the Sierras, a series of ditches, canals, and reservoirs made hydraulic mining possible. Water flowed into large iron pipes with even larger openings. Each pipe gradually narrowed until it reached an opening from four to six inches wide. Rushing from this opening under 300 to 400 feet of pressure, the water cut into the Sierra foothills like a surgeon's knife. Tons of earth

were blasted away from the mountainsides and washed toward miners eagerly waiting to extract the gold. What couldn't be unearthed by water pressure was blasted by kegs of black powder. Witnesses marveled at the awesome power of the hydraulic mines.

In 1870 Placer County Tax Assessor J.C. Boggs set the full assessed value of the county at $4,237,632.17. Taxes of $2.60 per $100 brought in $110,178.42 to the county treasury. As the nation celebrated its centennial in 1876, Placer County had $9,130.48 in its treasury, had paid all its bills, and owned all of its county buildings outright.

County officials during the 1870s were often paid by the amount of work completed instead of at a flat rate. The Placer County district attorney at that time could expect to be paid an annual salary of $500. For each conviction involving the death penalty, he received an additional $25. Felony convictions brought in an additional $12, and misdemeanor convictions were worth $8. The highest paid county official in 1870 was the sheriff, who earned $4,000 annually. Judges earned $2,000, the county clerk $3,000, the auditor $2,500, and the treasurer $1,500.

Life-styles did not always revolve around work. The mining towns were also known for their grand celebrations or, in some cases, lack of celebration. One such incident took place in Gold Run. In order to make the Fourth of July more enjoyable, the town put together a free public dinner. A 300-foot-long table was

placed down one side of Main Street. An estimated 500 people turned out to enjoy the celebration, with everything except whiskey provided free of charge. Within a short time the table was full and additional tables were put in place. Early in the celebration, it was realized that not enough roast meat had been cooked for the occasion. Knowing more had been purchased than eaten, the townspeople set out to discover who had stolen the meat. They came up empty-handed, and many partygoers went away hungry. The next day the meat was found, still in its shipping boxes, in the cellar of Harrison's Saloon, a fact not soon forgotten by many local pioneers.

As mining, the railroad, and agriculture continued to attract people to Placer County, its growth was reflected in the 1880 census. A total of 14,226 people lived in the county. Official records show 7,125 white males, 4,923 white females, 1,843 Chinese, 235 Colored, and 100 Indians. Once fast-growing mining towns like Elizabethtown, Wisconsin Hill, Illinoistown, Yorkville, Deadwood, Last Chance, and Sunny South were giving way to Iowa Hill, Michigan Bluff, Dutch Flat, and Colfax. Many local settlements still had little more than a post office, a general store, and a

blacksmith shop. Applegate is one settlement that was founded early and still remains today. First known as Lisbon, it was later named after G.W. Applegate, who was postmaster in the settlement for many years. Applegate has been credited with starting the summer resort business in Placer County.

Mining and railroading have always been a part of Placer County history, but agriculture most certainly deserves equal credit. As far back as 1859, when Mrs. J.R. Crandall was awarded a State Agriculture Society Award for best specimens of dried fruits at Sacramento's annual fair, agriculture was part of foothill living. It wasn't until 1886, however, that Placer County was recognized for its truly rich farming potential.

In December of that year Northern California counties organized a citrus fair in Sacramento. Auburn

Above: A train hauling lime-stone from the American River canyon crosses Mountain Quarries Bridge over the American River and begins its trip to Flint Station near Auburn. The railroad and bridge were in use between 1912 and 1942. Courtesy, Auburn Journal

Left: Before trucks were used to haul lumber and limestone, workers used literal horse-power methods. Courtesy, **Auburn Journal**

*Mining was the main industry
in Placer County from 1849 until the late 1890s. Hard rock,
placer, and hydraulic mining
were all common in the Sierra
foothills as the search for gold
continued throughout the second half of the century. Courtesy,*
Auburn Journal

*A group of Auburn area resi-
dents wait on the Auburn Stage
in the 1880s. Auburn Stage lines
provided transportation from
the county seat to other locations in the county. Courtesy,*
Auburn Journal

area residents, who had never before made a unified effort to participate in such an event, went about preparing for the competition. People not only went into the orchards, but they also picked fruit from the trees in their backyards. The results surprised not only Placer County residents but people from the surrounding counties as well. Placer County won first prize for "County Exhibit" at the State Fair. On Christmas Day 1886, a headline in the *Placer Herald* read "Semi-Tropical Placer." The county had won first, second, third, fourth, and fifth prizes for oranges from the Eden Ranch in the foothills. It also received recognition for its Royal Dehesa raisins. The exhibit met with such success that it was loaded into boxcars and sent to Chicago for display.

Enthusiasm over the citrus industry brought a Citrus Fair to Auburn in 1892. Auburn was one of three Northern California towns to host such an event, and its opera house afforded the space for the gala occasion. At about the same time olive planters began to recognize the high quality of crops produced in the foothills. Frederick Birdsall, Charles Reed, Emily Robinson, and F. Claus became well known for their olive crops. At first olives were grown for the single purpose of obtaining olive oil. A few years later, a new emphasis on growing whole olives as food changed the direction of the industry in the foothills.

The future of agriculture in Placer County at that time was directly tied to the price of shipping the food eastward. High shipping rates continued to hamper productivity in the Placer County area. Late in 1886 David Lubin was sent to New York to discuss lowering railroad shipping rates. On December 18 it was announced that railroad officials of the Central Pacific and Union Pacific would prorate fruit transportation. The reduction in rates meant that a 10-car instead of a 15-car train would leave Auburn and make faster time across the country. The cost per car to New York dropped from $800 to $400. The price of a trip to Chicago dropped from $600 to $300.

The prosperity brought by the railroads in the 1880s also brought a new kind of crime. Like earlier stage robberies, train robberies became a way of life in Placer County and Northern California. A rail of track could simply be removed, and the slow-moving trains derailed and easily robbed. Soon after the first incident of train wrecking, California law made it a crime that carried the death penalty on conviction.

One of the early Placer County cases went to court in 1881. On the night of September 1, a group of men attempted to rob the overland passenger train near Cape Horn above Colfax. After the robbers tore up a section of rail on the eastbound track, they attempted to rob the express car. They ordered the express clerk

Colfax, seen here in 1887, had a number of stores to help outfit miners as well as an increasing number of farmers in agricultural pursuits. Courtesy, **Auburn Journal**

Pictured here are guests of the Star Hotel at Iowa Hill in 1898. Courtesy, **Auburn Journal**

to hand over the money, but the doors were closed, and the robbers decided to leave rather than blow the doors off the car.

During the five trials that followed, suspect John Mason turned state's evidence and testified against the other four suspects. According to Mason the robbers heard that a group of soldiers had been seen getting off another car of the train and heading toward the express car. All five robbers fled, leaving behind giant powder cartridges, fuses, axes, sledges, and a battering ram. Word was carried to the Colfax telegraph office by a runner, and the authorities were notified. Sheriff John Boggs was assisted by the San Francisco police and railroad detectives in the search for the train robbers. The trail led to a cabin on the North Fork of the American River between Gold Run and Iowa Hill. With the suspects now in custody, the series of trials was the

talk of Auburn for several weeks. After the first suspects were convicted, the last trial was set to begin.

Prior to the first day in court, the judge ordered that Ed Steinegal, convicted in an earlier trial, be brought back from prison to testify as a witness. Sheriff Boggs boarded the train for Sacramento to bring Steinegal back that evening. Because of the State Fair the return train was crowded. As Boggs and his deputy escorted the handcuffed Steinegal down the ramp at Auburn Station, the convicted train robber cut in front of two young women and ran down an alley. He was never seen in Placer County again.

By the mid-1880s the residents of Auburn were once again working to incorporate the city. Since local voters had chosen to disincorporate in the early 1860s in order to avoid paying off the Sacramento, Placer, and Nevada Railroad bonds, little progress had been

This photograph shows the faculty and student body of the Sierra Normal College in 1888. Founded in 1882, the school was the first private normal school on the Pacific Coast and later became Placer County High School. Courtesy, **Auburn Journal**

made toward solving the problem. A series of negotiations produced a possible compromise. After over 25 years with no city government, Auburn once again became a city on May 2, 1888.

Schools, as well as the need for schools, continued to grow during this era. Schools were privately operated in the pioneer days, but public schools began to be established in the 1860s throughout Placer County. Many communities built their first school buildings in the 1870s as their populations grew. By the year 1881, 60 schoolteachers saw to the needs of the 2,947 students in the county. Of the students, 1,511 were boys and 1,436 girls. Auburn schools had the most students, with 257 attending daily. The Dutch Flat School had 205 students, and Colfax had 203. Those schools with more than 100 students included Rocklin (197), Foresthill (151), Ophir (137), Penryn (128), Iowa Hill

(125), Lincoln (105), and Roseville (103). School administration was conducted by 45 different school districts. At first students were required to attend school only 6.87 months a year. By the early 1900s, however, the school year had been increased to 10 months.

Education at the high school level was initially in the hands of Sierra Normal College, which was

*Right: Members of the Placer
Junior College football team
are seen in this 1936 photo.
Courtesy, Auburn Journal*

*Left: The Placer Herald is rec-
ognized as the oldest continuous
weekly newspaper in California.
Courtesy, Jim Johnson*

founded in 1882. Placer Union High School was organized in 1901. Its main buildings were constructed in 1906. The first organized high school athletic event attracted large numbers of spectators to see Placer face Sacramento High School in football. Placer won the contest 10-5 under the leadership of Coach E.S. Birdsall.

As East Auburn continued to grow, two new buildings were constructed during the 1890s. The first was the Auburn Opera House. After some debate over the need for a second opera house (one already existed in Old Town Auburn), the articles of incorporation of the Auburn Opera House and Pavilion Association were

*The belles of the Auburn Opera House are seen here circa the early 1900s. From left to right are: Francis Morgan, Dolly Morgan, Dorothy Staiger, Ruth James, Ruth Slade, Dorothy Lininger, and Lucille Waldo. Courtesy, **Auburn Journal***

filed on May 6, 1890. The following year 600 people packed the new structure for its opening night performance. Among the many people who traveled to Auburn for the opening was Governor Henry Markham. Until it was destroyed by fire on October 3, 1957, the opera house was a center of social activity. One of its most famous performers was John Philip Sousa, who appeared on November 2, 1907.

At about the same time, local residents and elected officials began to discuss the future of the county courthouse built in 1854. The structure was only wood, and most agreed it needed to be replaced. From the beginning the project was a hot topic, since some residents felt that it was too costly. The first attempts to obtain voter support resulted in bond elections in 1888 and 1890. Both elections failed to produce enough votes to approve the funding. At one point an effort was made to realign the county boundaries in order to secure voter support. For the next three years the Placer County Board of Supervisors collected a 5 percent tax to pay for the building. By October 1893 the supervisors had begun to search for an architect to design the

*Above: This 1918 photograph
shows Hotel Auburn on Lincoln
Way in East Auburn. The hotel
is still in use today and it is the
only remaining hotel in the city
that was used in the early
1900s. Courtesy, Auburn
Journal*

*Left: This Lower Auburn street
scene shows the Orleans Hotel
in the right rear. Courtesy,
Auburn Journal*

new structure. John M. Curtis was eventually selected and went to work on the design.

Once the design was accepted preliminary construction work was begun; on July 4, 1894, the laying of the cornerstone was celebrated. A copper box, which contained several gold coins, county newspapers, and artifacts, was placed inside the cornerstone. The day's activities included a parade, sports, and a series of speeches. The parade marched from the Freeman Hotel near the Auburn train station to the courthouse steps. Four years later, on July 4, the building was dedicated in front of an equally enthusiastic crowd. Judge J.E. Prewett officiated at the dedication following a parade. Highlighting the day were a balloon ascension and a parachute jump by the Hagal brothers.

Many Placer County residents were active Masons from the early pioneer days. The Masons, the Sons of Temperance, the Independent Order of Good Templars, the Improved Order of Red Men, the Patrons of Husbandry, and the Ancient Order of United Workmen were all active from the 1870s through the turn of the century.

Club activities also dominated the area's social life. One of the first clubs got its start in 1907, when the Tahoe Club was organized in Auburn. After using the Morgan Building for two years, the group built its own facility on the corner of High and East Placer streets. The upstairs was used for its club activities, and the downstairs was occupied by the Bell Electric Company. Hosting many social events, the Tahoe Club continues to exist today.

Another early community organization was the Auburn Improvement Club. It was organized in 1912, and its 103 members were led by their president, Mrs. J.M. Lowell. The group was established to elicit thought about and action for the benefit of Auburn, its people, and their social welfare. The group planted trees, built drinking fountains, erected historical landmarks, and attracted musical performers to the area.

During the early 1900s Auburn and Placer County bustled with growth. The area's busy life-style, however, was balanced by the presence of the Sierras. During the winter months only trains could connect East and West. Months would pass with all the mountain highways closed by deep snow. It was during these periods that the Central Pacific Railroad took on even more importance. Railroad stations became more than

Auburn Depot on Nevada Street was the stopping point for all west-bound passenger and freight trains. The station was built after the west-bound and east-bound rails were split, improving railroad safety in Placer County. Courtesy, **Auburn Journal**

Once known as East Auburn, this street scene, photographed in the early 1900s, shows several modes of transportation. Courtesy, **Auburn Journal**

just boarding points. For many Placer County communities the stations were also a link to the outside world when snow halted all other traffic.

Between Rocklin and Truckee lay 98.26 miles of track, along which the Central Pacific had 38 staff stations equipped with either a day and night telegraph office or day and night telephone capability. The greatest distance between staff stations on the line was 4.08 miles from the Tunnel 13 Station to the Eder Station. Today few people recognize station names like Troy, Tamarack, Smart, Gorge, Wirt, Lander, and Zeta. Yet in 1905 those stations played a major part in connect-

ing Sierra communities with those at lower elevations in Western Placer County.

Despite its importance to Placer County and the nation, the Central Pacific was having difficulties of its own. Corporate maneuvering within the railroad industry added the name "Southern Pacific Railroad" to the tracks over the Sierras. Beginning in 1884 the Southern Pacific leased the Central Pacific Railroad and continued to build railroads throughout the West. Taking full control of the Central Pacific on August 1, 1899, the Southern Pacific Company directed the operation of the line.

Fragmented ownership of a number of railroads between San Francisco and Chicago, including the financially troubled Union Pacific, ended when they were brought under one owner through the efforts of Edward Henry Harriman. Harriman invested over $45 million in the Union Pacific, making it one of the best-run and well-equipped railroads in the nation. Once he

One of the biggest construction projects in the early 1900s was the building of the Mountain Quarries Bridge. The railroad bridge over the American River was in use for nearly 40 years. Courtesy, **Auburn Journal**

obtained control of the Union Pacific through auction, he turned his attention west to the Central Pacific. The death of the Central Pacific's Collis Huntington in August 1900 gave Harriman the opportunity to gain control of the Central Pacific. Within a year Harriman was elected president of the Southern Pacific Railroad.

Once in power he turned his attention toward the many problems faced by the railroad between Rocklin and Truckee. For the most part the track running through Placer County was the original track that had been built in the 1860s. Single tracks slowed east-west

travel. Tunnels were small and train trestles hazardous. Harriman, who believed in the value of the railroad to national commerce, saw the tracks running through Placer County as the key to growth. Under his leadership $240 million was spent on new equipment, reconstruction, and new tracks over the Sierras. Harriman died in September 1909, before most of the work was completed. His plans for the railroad, however, continued on with a number of major improvements that are still in use today.

From Sacramento to the summit of the Sierras, the tracks climbed 7,032 feet. Between Newcastle and Colfax construction began on a number of double tracks, which eliminated the problem of eastbound and westbound trains having to wait on sidings for each other to pass. Along the westbound track, Tunnels 18, 19, and 20 were drilled and a new 540-foot trestle was constructed over Auburn Ravine. A few miles east of Auburn, between Bowman and Applegate, construct-

ing double tracking became more difficult because of the grade, but with the construction of Tunnels 22, 23, 24, and 25 near Applegate, which were completed by April 18, 1911, the second track became fully operational.

As new tunnels, tracks, and trains appeared, control of the railroad was again challenged. In 1913 the U.S. Supreme Court ordered the Union Pacific to divest itself of all Southern Pacific stock. A year later the government attempted to separate the Southern Pacific from the Central Pacific. While battles over control of the railroads were being fought in the courts, track improvements stopped. At the same time use of the railroads increased. During 1913, 18 passenger trains made the trip from Sacramento to Sparks, Nevada, each day.

Crossing the American River between Placer and El Dorado counties was not an easy task. A number of bridges were built, including this toll bridge below Auburn. Courtesy, **Auburn Journal**

While railroads met the travel and commercial needs of Placer County and the nation, aviation was just getting off the ground. It arrived in Placer County just eight years after the Wright brothers flew at Kitty Hawk, North Carolina. R.G. Fowler landed his Wright biplane just east of Auburn on September 11, 1911,

R.G. Fowler lands his Wright biplane near the Southern Pacific Railroad depot on Nevada Street in Auburn on September 11, 1911. Fowler was attempting to be the first man to fly from the West Coast to New York and win the $50,000 offered by William Randolph Hearst. After several attempts he failed to get past Blue Canyon. He later had his biplane taken by train to Los Angeles where he flew to Florida in 45 days. Courtesy, **Auburn Journal**

near the Southern Pacific Railroad station on Nevada Street. Fowler became known as the Placer County "Bird Man" because of his attempts to fly from San Francisco to New York and become the first man to make the flight over the Sierras. Circling the Placer County Courthouse, Fowler landed in Collins' field. On hand to meet the aviator were his old friends Percy Root, A.J. Barclay, John T. Walsh, who later became mayor of Auburn, and the president of the Auburn Chamber of Commerce, William G. Lee. While Fowler spent the night at the Freeman Hotel in Auburn, local townspeople took turns standing watch over his aircraft.

Fowler was attempting to collect a $50,000 prize for being the first person to complete the west-to-east flight to New York before October 11, 1911. The money was offered by William Randolph Hearst. For two weeks Fowler tried to climb over the Sierras; each time strong winds, mechanical trouble, and the weather forced him to crash or land the aircraft. Eventually, after making it as far as Emigrant Gap, he loaded the Wright biplane onto a Southern Pacific flatcar for the trip back to Auburn.

Realizing he couldn't make the October 11 deadline, Fowler continued his flight, but decided to travel south before crossing the Sierras. Leaving from Los Angeles Fowler reached Florida 45 days later. He thus became the second pilot to cross the country and the first to do it from west to east. After becoming the first man to bring aviation to Placer County, Fowler became a resident of San Jose, where he died in June 1966 at the age of 83.

Chapter
IV

Roads and Rails Spur Growth

1917-1945

World War I brought with it the Selective Service Law, which was passed on May 18, 1917. The registration of men between 21 and 31 years of age began in Placer County on June 5, under the direction of Placer County Clerk Marshall Z. Lowell. In order to make the new draft law work, the Placer County Council of Defense established the first Exemption Board, made up of W.B. Hotchkiss of Applegate, W.D. Ingram of Lincoln, and H.E. Butler of Penryn. Meeting for the first time at 3 p.m. on July 1 in the Placer County Courthouse, the Exemption Board began the process of classifying those who had registered. Physical examinations for the draft were first given on August 3, 1917, with 100 to 150 Auburn area men being examined daily.

A year later the second call for draft registration in Placer County took place on June 5, 1918. The registration age was lowered to 18, and another 3,086 names were added to the list. The total number of draft-age men on the Placer County Exemption Board lists was 4,929 during World War I. Under the leadership of the provost marshal general, Auburn's draft quota on August 10, 1917, was 165 men. As they left the area for military training, the men were honored by large gatherings of area leaders and friends. The first group was made up of leader John L. Shannon, Lawrence J. Dunn, Charles Bond, Guiseppe del Debbio, Owen Pryterch, Albert H. Long, Alfred H. Fowler, and Thomas R. Jones. The men were honored at a special luncheon at the Hotel Auburn. Among those people in attendance was California Governor William D. Stephens, who greeted each draftee with a handshake and wished him Godspeed. Of the first draftees del Debbio was the only one to be killed in action. By the end of the year, 228 Placer County men had left for the battlefront. By the end of the war, 416 Placer County men had been drafted, and another 150 had enlisted. Some, however, enlisted before being called to duty. Estimates place the number of county men serving in World War I at 600 to 700, with the greatest number coming from Auburn.

The Placer County war effort was not restricted to supplying men for the military. Throughout World War I, since the county agricultural explosion was in high gear, the area played a major role in supplying fresh fruit to the military and civilian populations. Having formed the Pacific Fruit Express in 1906, the Southern Pacific and the Union Pacific opened one of the largest precooling plants in the country in Roseville in 1909. With the help of a new vacuum process, the Roseville operation could reduce the temperature of 24 cars from 80 to 40 degrees in two hours. The plant produced 250 tons of ice a day. During the war the time it took fruit trains to travel from Roseville to Sparks was reduced to 17 hours.

The number of fruit blocks (10 or more fruit cars) continued to grow as the war raged on. By 1919 Roseville had sent 567 fruit blocks over the Sierras.

Left: The Placer County Court-house, built north of Lower Auburn in the 1890s, stands out against the horizon. This photograph was taken shortly after the 1905 Washington Street fire, with Auburn in the foreground. The foundations of some of the burned buildings can also be seen in the foreground. Courtesy, **Auburn Journal**

Below: Auburn's first Southern Pacific railroad depot was located in East Auburn at the foot of Lincoln Way, which was known at that time as Railroad Street. The station operated until the 1970s. It was purchased by the City of Auburn in 1988 for its Centennial celebration. Courtesy, **Auburn Journal**

Turlock had processed 44, and other areas of the state, such as Los Angeles, had produced another 237 fruit blocks. Under wartime conditions the United States Railway Administration added 52 additional fruit trains, and all of them were Western Pacific fruit blocks that traveled over the mountains.

Following the war attention once again shifted to completing the double tracking of the Southern Pacific tracks over the Sierras. The final section of the second track was completed near the summit in 1925, and 242 miles of double track stretched from Oakland to Sparks, mostly through Placer County.

Two years later, in 1921, economic conditions in Placer County began to reflect the difficult times seen across the country. Since the railroad was one of the largest employers in the county, the Placer County economy mirrored railroad trends. During the summer of 1929 an estimated 1,360 men worked in the

Roseville Southern Pacific shops and yards. Two years later nearly one third of those men were without work. The Colfax roundhouse was closed, and 33 men were laid off in 1930. One by one the freight and passenger trains through Placer County and over the Sierras were reduced in number.

At the same time, automobile travel over the Sierras increased. For three years, between 1929 and 1931, travelers could drive their cars onto baggage cars dur-

Above: DeWitt Military Hospital is seen here shortly after construction during World War II. The hospital served many veterans returning from the front lines in the Pacific. It was later a state mental hospital, and today is owned and operated by Placer County as a government center. Courtesy, **Auburn Journal**

Steam locomotives and rail service was in its heyday in the 1920s. This 1923 photo of the Southern Pacific station and yard in Colfax shows its involvement in railroading. Courtesy, **Auburn Journal**

ing the winter months for the trip between Sacramento and Reno.

For the first time, however, more and more local residents weren't as interested in getting through the snow as in getting to it. The winter sports industry was drawing an increasing amount of attention to Placer County.

Skiing in California actually had its beginnings during the Gold Rush, when miners fashioned home-made skis during the winter months while the snow kept them away from mining. These isolated attempts to ski didn't begin to resemble the modern sport until 1928, when Wendell Robie and a group of Auburn residents formed the Auburn Ski Club.

When the snows arrived in the Sierras, most people simply packed up and moved below the snowline at 3,500 feet. Except for the railroad, nothing moved in the Sierras once the snow arrived.

During 1928, however, members of the Auburn Ski Club selected a site three miles east of Towle on Old Highway 40 and built California's first modern ski jump. After obtaining permission from the Placer County Board of Supervisors for the ski jump, which both parties thought was on county land, Robie soon received notification that the property belonged to the Pacific Gas & Electric Company (PG&E). Since the club

*This 1918 photograph shows
Auburn area residents waiting
at "Round Corner" for the motor stage. Located at the intersection of Main and Washington streets, the corner got its
name because of the round
architecture of the building.
Courtesy,* **Auburn Journal**

was unwilling to accept the fact that the group might
have to move its ski jump, it met with PG&E officials.
Realizing the service skiers could provide PG&E by
reaching downed power lines in snow areas, PG&E
became a strong supporter of the Auburn Ski Club and
its activities. Soon the Auburn Ski Club was the largest
organization of its kind west of the Mississippi. Out of
its organizational efforts came the Far West California
Ski Association.

Skiing, however, really began to gain statewide
attention in 1931, when the Auburn Ski Club, with the
help of one of its members, Senator Bert A. Cassidy,
convinced other state legislators to provide enough
money to keep Highway 40 clear of snow during the
winter months. Since they believed in the potential of
winter sports in California, members of the Auburn
Ski Club invited all the members of the legislature to
spend a day in the snow. Leaving Auburn at 6 a.m. on
January 18, 1931, a caravan of 56 cars went to Sacramento to pick up the elected officials and their families.

At the same time the selling point for providing
snow removal was that the extra gas taxes generated
would more than pay for the cost of the project. Trying
to generate automobile traffic along the one-way section of Highway 40 already cleared of snow, Auburn
Ski Club members also invited local residents to see a

free ski jumping event held while the legislators were at
the ski jump. Everyone had a good time on that January day, according to reports in the *Auburn Journal*, and
California Highway Patrol reports indicated that 2,400
automobiles were crowded along the narrow stretch of
highway for the ski jump exhibition. The next day the
California legislature passed a bill providing for snow
clearance on Highway 40 over the summit.

Robie and the Auburn Ski Club, however, were just
beginning. In 1932 the United States Ski Championships were held at Lake Tahoe. In May of that year, following the successful completion of the championships, the club received a letter from a young man
named Roy Mikkelsen. Mikkelsen, who lived in Madi-
son, Wisconsin, had participated in the event. Because
of the Depression and the scarcity of jobs in Wisconsin,
he wanted to know if he could get a job in California.
Auburn Lumber Company offered him a job piling
lumber, and Mikkelsen was soon living in Placer

*Below: World War II proved to
be the busiest time in history for
the Southern Pacific Railroad
route through Placer County.
This steam engine was one of
dozens to pass through Colfax on
a daily basis as war needs
required a great amount of men
and material to be shipped both
east and west. Courtesy,*
Auburn Journal

*Right: Wendell T. Robie, born
on May 28, 1895, was the presi-
dent of Hearst Federal Savings
& Loan Association, charter
president of the Auburn Ski
Club, and a member of the U.S.
Olympic Games Committee.
Robie died October 31, 1984.
Courtesy,* **Auburn Journal**

County. He went on to win two U.S. Ski Jump Championships, become a member of two U.S. Olympic
teams, serve as a combat infantry officer during World
War II, distinguish himself as mayor of Auburn, own
shares of the Auburn Lumber Company, and hold a
directorship of the Federal Savings and Loan Association.

During the same period, skiing moved to a new ski
area on Mt. McIntosh near Cisco. From 1933 until the
beginning of World War II, the downhill race from Mt.
McIntosh became the championship event for California skiers. Still the sport needed additional participants. Dr. Joel Hildebrand, a Nobel Prize winner in
chemistry from the University of California, Berkeley,
began to study snow behavior. Auburn Ski Club members hauled a truckload of snow to Berkeley, where it
was discovered the snow did not melt as fast as most
people expected.

61

On the basis of that information, the Auburn Ski Club was sanctioned to hold what was called the San Francisco Bay Ski Jumping Championships in Berkeley. Civilian Conservation Corps (CCC) members shoveled eight large gondola carloads of snow on a Southern Pacific train for the trip to Berkeley. Once the snow was in the Bay Area, another group of CCC members shoveled it onto a steep hill at the foot of Hearst Avenue. The event received press coverage throughout the state, including 2,000 column inches in Bay Area newspapers alone. An estimated 100,000 spectators were on hand for the ski jump championships in Berkeley.

Following the success of that event, organizers of the Golden Gate International Exposition, which was to be held on Treasure Island, contacted the Auburn Ski Club in 1938 to see if a similar ski jumping event could be part of the exposition. A 185-foot ski jump was built on Treasure Island; and, with the help of the Union Ice Company, which had developed a machine that could make snow out of ice, ski jumping was part of the two-year exposition. Among the guests of the Auburn Ski Club on the opening day of the event was future California Governor Earl Warren.

Back in the Sierras, Auburn Ski Club members set about constructing a chapel at the club's Winter Park at Cisco. With the help of Father Richard Vereker from St. Joseph's Catholic Church in Auburn, a call went out

for a skiing chaplain. Father Bracken soon found himself learning the art of snow skiing.

World War II turned the attention of the Auburn Ski Club from winter sports to recruiting and training military units that could fight in the snow-covered Appenines and Alps of Italy. Auburn Ski Club members helped to form the U.S. Army 10th Mountain Division's 85th, 86th, and 87th regiments. They not only were a part of the unit but trained others to ski under battlefield conditions. Japan's attack on Pearl Harbor, Hawaii, on December 7, 1941, met with immediate response in Placer County. Not only did the area have a large population of American citizens of Japanese descent, but it was believed that the passage of the Southern Pacific Railroad through the county made the area a major military target in the event of further hostilities.

Fear of hysteria and racial prejudice led the Placer County Defense Council, under the direction of District Attorney Lowell Sparks, to issue a statement calling for full cooperation and restraint on the part of all citizens, irrespective of birth or descent. The message of calm was printed on the front page of the December 8, 1941, issue of the *Auburn Journal*.

Following the Sunday attack few Placer County residents slept as meetings were held well into the night. Among the groups dealing with the U.S. entry

These skiers enjoy the facilities and the slopes at Squaw Valley. Photo by Mark E. Gibson

These flags greet visitors to Squaw Valley, site of the 1960 Winter Olympics. Photo by Mark E. Gibson

into World War II on the night of the attack were the Placer County Defense Council, the Auburn Chapter of the American Red Cross, Company E of the 184th Infantry of the California State Guard in Auburn, the Placer County Japanese-American Citizens League (JACL), and all local law enforcement agencies. Placer County Sheriff Charles Silva posted special guards at vital defense points in the county and had the railroad tracks patrolled to prevent sabotage.

At the time of the attack, it was estimated that the population of people with Japanese ancestry in the county included 300 members of the JACL, 200 nonmembers, 700 American-born Japanese residents under the age of 21, and an additional 700 Japanese aliens. A statement prepared by the JACL and presented by JACL President George Sakamoto was published December 8 in the *Auburn Journal*. The statement read as follows:

> *The news of war has come to me as a great shock and surprise. In issuing this statement, I am proud that I am an American citizen and at this time of extreme National Emergency, I wish to reiterate the statements that I have made and reassure you that we Americans of Japanese extraction are 100 percent behind the National Defense Program, and that we are undivided in our loyalty to the Stars and Stripes. There are now more than 2,500 of our boys in the armed services of the United States who are proving to be good soldiers. Now that we must face the grim reality of this war, I wish to take this means to plead for your tolerance and fair play through the duration of the conflict.*

The week following the attack, activities related to civil defense continued at a brisk pace. Members of the Auburn Volunteer Fire Department completed work on a map for blackouts within the community. Members of the Richard W. Townsend Post of the American Legion began a campaign for volunteers to assist in the defense effort. Within four days of the attack on Pearl

Not all activities of the Auburn Volunteer Fire Department were aimed at putting out fires. Since being formed in 1852, the Auburn Volunteer Fire Department has served the community in many ways. During some events, a number of games tested the skills of the Auburn department and its East Auburn counterpart. The two fire departments eventually joined forces under one fire board. Courtesy, Auburn Journal

Harbor, 19 men from the area had joined the Auburn unit of the California State Guard. Auburn also experienced its first blackout from 8 p.m. until 11 p.m. on December 8. Those people who did not observe the blackout faced arrest. Citizens were told by Auburn Police Chief Joe Hamilton to stay off the streets during blackouts.

By December 18, 1941, the Placer County Defense Council had also received word to prepare to accept evacuees in Placer County if it became necessary to remove citizens from larger cities. G.W. Brundage, who was in charge of the Disaster Relief Committee, said

Auburn could house and feed 2,500 evacuees if necessary. Within two weeks of Pearl Harbor, Auburn civic leader Eleanor Lukens reported that 500 area residents had volunteered to work on civil defense projects in Auburn. The Placer Defense Council also opened its new office in the Walsh Building on Maple Street.

Efforts to identify aliens began to take shape in January as the Department of Justice ordered all German, Italian, and Japanese aliens to register between February 2 and 7. At its February 5 meeting, the Placer County Board of Supervisors passed a resolution asking that all enemy aliens be removed from Placer County. At the same time the draft once again began the process of identifying those young men eligible for military service. It was estimated that 2,200 to 2,500 would register in Placer County.

Civil defense took on a military guise as Placer rifle units were established in each community under the leadership of the district attorney and the sheriff. The rifle units were to be used in case of enemy attacks within California.

By early March General J.L. DeWitt, who commanded the Western Defense Command and the Fourth Army, had issued a proclamation to all Japanese Americans and enemy aliens in the area. The proclamation set an 8 p.m. to 6 a.m. curfew for the Japanese and made it illegal for them to own or have firearms. DeWitt advised local Japanese Americans to settle property rights, dispose of businesses, and

Above: Colfax Fire Department volunteers take time out to be photographed with their "new" fire truck in the 1920s. It was one of the Colfax Volunteer Fire Department's first motorized fire trucks. Courtesy, **Auburn Journal**

Right: The Auburn Semi-Pro Baseball Team regularly played games with neighboring teams. Courtesy, **Auburn Journal**

arrange for the handling of their farms, pointing out that they might be relocated at any time.

After many weeks of talk about Japanese relocation efforts, the plan went into effect May 11, when 2,000 local Japanese residents were ordered to report to the local Control Stations in Newcastle and Loomis. The May 14 issue of the *Auburn Journal* reported that all the Japanese within Military Area One in Placer County had been removed to a location near Marysville. In the absence of the skills contributed by the Japanese, plans were also put into motion to bring in volunteers from San Francisco area schools to help increase the labor force in the Placer County orchards.

While the war news was not good, the citizens of Auburn held an "On to Victory Day" celebration on April 25, 1942. Included in the activities were a parade, a dance, speeches, and a special War Bond Drive. Over $50,000 in War Bonds were sold during the day, as well as $500 in War Stamps. Applications also began for war ration books. The war effort also produced a number of material shortages, and over 50 tons of old rubber were collected from local residents. The rubber was recycled for war use.

One of the first Auburn servicemen to be decorated for gallantry in World War II was Lieutenant Donald Graham. Graham received the Silver Star for gallantry in action while flying one of the first B-17 bombers over a Japanese base on Rabaul, New Britain, on October 9, 1942. Graham's aircraft was one of the first over the base. He dropped flares for following bombers to use in pinpointing the target.

One of the best-known local war heroes was Major Clarence Anderson of Newcastle. Anderson was credited with shooting down 19 1/2 German planes during the war. The American Ace flew a P-51 fighter named "Old Crow" throughout the war.

Military buildup in Placer County continued. Following the construction of the DeWitt Military Hospital in North Auburn, plans took shape in April 1945 to establish a prisoner of war facility at Camp Flint near the Auburn Fairgrounds and the present Auburn Dam overlook. Approximately 200 to 300 German prisoners were brought to the POW camp to assist with groundskeeping and maintenance duties at DeWitt Hospital. Camp Flint had been used earlier as the base for the 754th Military Police Battalion, Ninth Service Command. The unit was disbanded in 1943.

DeWitt Hospital officials reported in the *Auburn Journal* on April 26, 1945, that the hospital had 1,688 patients, 551 enlisted personnel (including 109 WACs), 299 officers, and 537 civilian employees.

To celebrate the end of the war, local residents gathered at the Placer County Courthouse on August 15 for an address by Superior Court Judge Lowell Sparks. Sparks called on Placer County residents to observe the golden rule following the greatest war the world had ever seen. After a number of speeches a victory parade took place through downtown Auburn.

Lower Auburn, as it appeared in 1896, is seen here from the dome of the Placer County Courthouse. While many of the buildings in the left side of the photo remain today, most of those on the right side of the photograph were either destroyed by the fire in 1905 or removed for highway construction. Courtesy, Auburn Journal

Chapter V

New
Foothills
Migration

1946-1987

World War II had brought many changes to Auburn and to Placer County. During the last five months of 1945, life in the foothills was a great deal like that in other sections of the country, as communities welcomed home the men and women who had gone off to war. Early in 1946, however, a number of decisions were made that would affect area residents in the decades to come.

First, military officials closed down DeWitt Hospital, named for General DeWitt, on December 31, 1945. Local efforts to have the hospital turned over to the Veteran's Administration failed. Auburn, VA officials said, was too far away from major population centers to be used for a veterans hospital. Next, area politicians turned to state officials in hopes the facility could be a state hospital. At the same time Camp Flint remained under the control of the army, since both German and Italian prisoners of war were still in Auburn. Delays in turning Camp Flint over to the Twentieth District Agricultural District resulted in an announcement by Bert Cassidy, recently re-elected president of the board of directors, that no fair would be held in Auburn in 1946.

With the war behind everyone, attention turned to the future. Returning veterans created a shortage of homes, and planners began the post-war building boom. In order to bring natural gas to Auburn, Pacifc Gas and Electric officials pledged $1.25 million for the construction of a pipeline from the existing one run-

ning between Lincoln and Roseville. Natural gas arrived in homes and businesses in the Auburn area for the first time in the fall of 1946. Less than a year after the atomic bomb was dropped, bringing an end to World War II, Auburn residents were beginning to hear the term "nuclear age." In early May Placer College science instructor Harold Weaver held a community forum to talk about the bomb and the changes it had brought. "Now that we have the bomb," Weaver said, "mass murder is inevitable in the event of another war. The scientific achievement can and must be put to peacetime use to make war unnecessary. It then seems fair to say that the studies in atomic energy have made war unnecessary and intolerable."

Medical science also came to Auburn in 1946, when the California Department of Mental Hygiene took over the DeWitt Hospital complex as a facility for aged and/or senile mental patients. Three months later the first 100 male patients arrived at DeWitt from the Napa Mental Hospital.

Auburn's two fire departments, uptown's Hook and Ladder Company No. 1 and downtown's Hose Company No. 2, agreed to merge into one Auburn Volunteer Fire Department under the direction of a single board. As 1946 came to a close, Guy Lukens, who had been Auburn fire chief for the past 41 years, retired. Henry Gietzen, who had served as first assistant under Lukens, became fire chief. Gietzen continued to serve as chief through 1987.

*Above: Highway 40 winds
through Roseville, Auburn, and
Colfax, climbing into the Sierras
toward Lake Tahoe and Reno.
Courtesy,* **Auburn Journal**

City planners had produced the first Auburn zoning map by December 1946. The planners assigned each piece of property inside the city a designation of commercial, industrial, single family, or multiple family. A map of the new zoning was published in the *Auburn Journal* on December 12.

Another change that took place during the months following World War II involved the use and control of Auburn Airport. It was closed by the military except for emergency landings during the war years. The Civil Aeronautics Authority (CAA) made plans to close it down completely after the war, but Horace "Ace" Hibbard spearheaded an effort in Auburn to raise local money to purchase the facility from the government. Hibbard was able to raise the $10,200 needed by the city to purchase the airport. A check for that amount was presented to City Councilman Ray Carlisle in November as the city continued negotiations with CAA authorities.

1946 also saw a 25 percent increase in Auburn property taxes, and Placer County as a whole reported an assessed valuation that year of $41,121,005. A new census was being taken as 1946 came to an end, which was sure to show an increase from the 1941 census figure of 4,013 Auburn residents.

Public support for the preservation of Auburn's heritage surfaced in early 1951, while the city council was deciding whether to replace the firehouse in Old Town Auburn. Many local residents were unhappy be-cause a fountain in the historic section of the city had been removed without public participation in the decision. When the city council put the firehouse matter before the public during its regular meeting in March, a large protest by residents against the building's destruction ended with no decision by the council; instead, a committee was formed to study the possibility of saving the structure. While the council said it did not want to destroy the historic firehouse, it also did not have the funds to repair it. Recommendations by the committee to save the structure were supported by the city council. A fire on August 14, 1951, however, almost destroyed the firehouse before it could be saved. Several businesses were lost in the blaze, and the roof of the firehouse was slightly burned, but the building survived. It was later restored and moved to a new location a block away, where it continues to be a well-known Auburn landmark.

A decline in business in 1951 was blamed on the routing of Highway 40 traffic around the downtown

This plant in Lincoln was the largest clay producing plant west of Chicago. All kinds of sewer pipes, tiling, flower pots, and pressed brick were produced, employing several hundred men year round. Courtesy, Placer County Chamber of Commerce

*Right: City maintenance workers make road repairs where California and Bordman intersect, two blocks from city hall.
Courtesy,* **Auburn Journal**

Left: Plaza Fountain in Historic Auburn was a popular landmark for many years. Courtesy, **Auburn Journal**

area, rather than along the old route on Lincoln Way. Plans to make the bypass even larger continued during the early 1950s because many sections of the highway between Sacramento and the Nevada state line were only two lanes wide. Money, or the lack of it, was the issue, as federal and state authorities said they couldn't afford the improvements.

Snow in the Sierras gained national attention early in 1952, when a storm said to be the worst in 62 years pounded the mountains. The streamliner *City of San Francisco,* with 226 people aboard, became stuck in the snow near Nyack. Efforts to send snow removal engines along the snowbound track to rescue the passengers failed as winter closed in on the stranded train. A short distance from the track, Highway 40 was also closed in both directions by heavy snow and a truck

The Placer County Bank was one of the first banks in the area and continues in operation on Lincoln Way. Courtesy, **Auburn Journal**

accident. Making the situation even more difficult, wire services picked up the story and broadcast it nationwide, including the history of the Donner Party and the fate of those party members who died while trapped in the snow. Finally the weather began to cooperate. After the *City of San Francisco* had spent four days trapped in the snow, a rescue group using a Pacific Gas and Electric snowcat reached the train. At the same time road crews were able to clear a path from Nyack Lodge at Emigrant Gap to a point just below the snowbound train.

Members of the first rescue teams to reach the stranded passengers reported that conditions were critical. The fuel that had kept the train's engine running and providing heat to the passengers had run out. Without heat, water pipes in the train were rupturing, and toilets were frozen. Women and children had used pillowcases with holes cut out for their eyes to help keep their faces warm. Wrapped in blankets, the passengers were led down a narrow path to waiting cars on Highway 40. From there they were taken back to Emi-

grant Gap and loaded onto a rescue train. Just after 9 p.m. on January 16, 1952, the transfer of all passengers was completed, and the rescue train began to travel west to lower elevations.

A second storm, however, stalled the opening of rail service over the Sierras. It wasn't until January 27 that train service was back to normal. Highway 40 wasn't opened for use until early February. Changes were also taking place in the rail industry, because the blizzard of 1952 had proven the superiority of diesel locomotives over the steam-driven trains of the 1930s and 1940s.

Sports enthusiasm grew in Placer County to match that of the early 1930s, providing the thrust needed for improving highway conditions. The combination of the Winter Olympic Games scheduled for February 1960 in Squaw Valley and the 1956 Highway Act produced today's modern interstate highway through Placer County.

After five years of plans but no money for widening Highway 40, the Federal Highway Act provided the

*Above: On January 14, 1952,
the City of San Francisco
Streamliner was stuck in the
snow near Emigrant Gap. It
took three days for rescue teams
to reach the stranded train and
the 226 people on board. While
none of the passengers died in
the incident, one Southern Pacific employee was killed during
efforts to reach the snowbound
train. Courtesy, Auburn
Journal*

*Right: Construction on Inter-
state 80 is seen in this 1958 ae-
rial photo. Courtesy, Auburn
Journal*

funding for the new freeway, renamed Highway 80, to
be built. Every effort was made to complete the four-
lane freeway project from Sacramento to Truckee in
time for the Olympic Games. Records showed that the
average snow pack at the summit was 10 feet; during
the blizzard of 1952, the snow pack had reached a
depth of 26 feet. With a projected average daily traffic
count of 5,500 vehicles, of which 12 percent would be
trucks, the new interstate route was designed with snow
and wind conditions in mind. Efforts to design it were

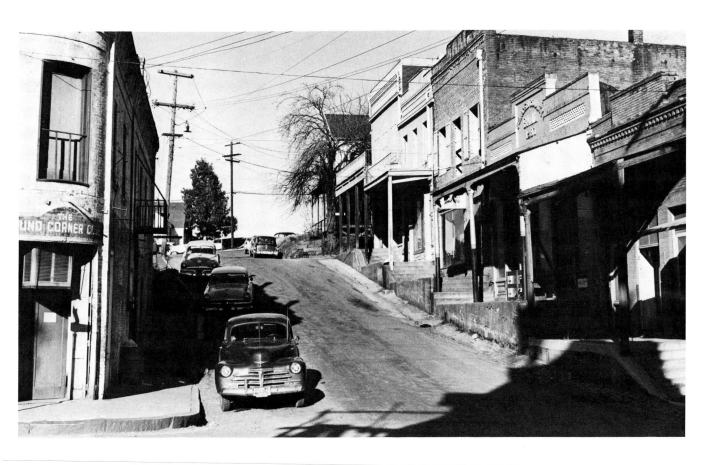

Commercial Street in Historic Auburn is seen here in the early 1950s prior to major restoration of the area. Courtesy, **Auburn Journal**

aimed at reducing the cost of snow removal and increasing safety, and it was built for a design speed of 60 miles per hour. Construction of the new project began along the 5.8-mile section of Highway 80 between Colfax and Gold Run. Throughout the 1950s work continued until completion of the freeway in 1961.

State Route 89 between Highway 80 and Squaw Valley was finished in 1959. It provided modern highway access to the Olympic Village, and the 8.3-mile section was opened in time for the Winter Olympic Games.

Auburn, the county seat for Placer County, took over the DeWitt complex in 1971. Assembly Bill 1740 was passed May 18, transferring the DeWitt State Hospital to the county. With the hospital no longer in oper-

ation, the DeWitt complex was operated under the DeWitt Development Authority. In addition to housing many government offices, it is also used by private industry and many community organizations. Located in North Auburn, the complex is situated on 225 acres.

One of the most controversial projects ever proposed for Auburn and for Placer County was the Auburn Dam on the American River. Officially the project got underway on September 2, 1965, as part of the U.S. Bureau of Reclamation's Central Valley Project. The Auburn Dam was supposed to be built 32 miles northeast of Sacramento, just below Auburn. It was designed to be a double-curvature concrete arch dam 685 feet high, 40 feet thick at the top, 190 feet wide at the base, and 4,150 feet across. If completed, it would have been the longest dam in the world and would have boasted a four-lane freeway connecting Placer and El Dorado counties. It would have created a water reservoir with a surface area of 10,000 acres, holding 2,300,000 acre-feet of water. Recreational use would have stretched 25 miles upstream on the North and Middle forks of the American River, once popular locations for Placer County gold mining. In addition to meeting the needs of the California water plan, it would have included a plant capable of generating 522 million kilowatt hours of electricity annually.

The Auburn Dam project was supported by Auburn business leaders and the city government. Once congressional approval was received, it was estimated it would take 18 months to complete the design of the dam and another six and one-half years to build

Although plans for Auburn Dam were completed in the early 1970s, construction was stalled due to financial restraints and concern for earthquake standards. Seen here is an artist's conception of the project. Courtesy, U.S. Bureau of Reclamation

it. A series of delays and mounting controversy slowed the project. By 1977, 75 percent of the excavation and foundation work had been completed. A diversion tunnel carried the American River underground and past the construction site.

Designed to provide water storage, hydroelectric power, and flood control for the Sacramento Basin, the project faced one roadblock after another during the early period of construction. The cost of the project during this period climbed from $500 million to $1 billion. When it appeared the money would be made available, concern over earthquake activity and the effects it would have on the project sent designers back to the drawing board for additional environmental studies. Several volumes of information on earthquake faults in the Auburn area, mineralization, and foundation studies had been prepared and reviewed by 1977. Yet the project continued to be stalled.

Dry Creek Road in North Auburn was often flooded following heavy rains and rising creek waters. Courtesy, **Auburn Journal**

Then, after the environmental issues had been resolved, funding was stopped. Early in February 1977 President Jimmy Carter announced the Auburn Dam was one of 19 water projects nationwide that he was recommending be cut from the Federal Budget.

For the next nine years debates over funding halted all work on the Auburn Dam. Even the election of former California Governor Ronald Reagan as president did little to put the project back on track.

It wasn't until the winter of 1986 that the Auburn Dam project was given new life. Supporters of the flood-control potential of the project made their point during the week of February 16, as a warm Pacific storm moved over Northern California. Over 12 inches of warm rain pelted the foothills in four days. The rain melted the snow at higher elevations, sending water thundering down the North and Middle forks of the American River. The canyon quickly filled, covering the Highway 49 Bridge between Auburn and Cool. Two days later the water began to crest the 230-foot coffer dam built to divert water under the Auburn Dam project. The cresting water eroded the earth-filled surfaces of the dam, collapsing it and sending 118,000 acre-feet of water down the American River

into Folsom Lake. That night another 4.85 inches of rain fell on Auburn. City streets were under water, and many buildings and homes were flooded as storm drains began to crack under the pressure of the water.

Downstream, plans were made to evacuate thousands of Sacramento area residents from lower areas if the rain did not stop. Just after midnight the rain began to let up. The storm had passed, but experts predicted just six more hours of rain would have required more water to be let out of Folsom Lake than the levee system could have handled. The loss of life and property, experts said, would have been high. Officially the storm claimed the lives of three Placer County residents, caused $10 million worth of damage in Placer County and another $2 million worth in Auburn, and swept away the Auburn coffer dam. Highway 49 between Auburn and Cool was washed away when the dam broke, and it took months to rebuild the route.

With the storm over, Auburn Dam supporters attracted the interest of Sacramento politicians, who were faced with solving the flood-control problems demonstrated during the storm. The high cost of flood insurance for those people below the American River also became a major political problem. It appeared the

Left: One of the most popular events held in Auburn is the annual sidewalk sale and fair. The event, held each spring, attracts thousands of shoppers and vendors. Courtesy, **Auburn Journal**

Below: The Historic Placer County Courthouse was designed and built in the 1890s. Courtesy, **Auburn Journal**

construction of the Auburn Dam would once again get underway.

Another year of study, hearings, and meetings at the local, state, and federal levels produced a plan calling for the construction of a flood-control dam at the Auburn site. Sacramento political leaders, in supporting the dam concept, called for the dam to be kept dry and only used for flood control during peak rainy seasons.

Construction of the Auburn Dam, this time for power generation and water conservation, once again faced a roadblock. Supporters of the project continued to work to get it going. The prospect of that happening as 1987 came to a close remained remote. Once again the 20-year-old Auburn Dam project was stalled.

While the dam was stalled, efforts that had begun in 1976 to restore the Placer County Courthouse continued into 1988. Dedicated on July 4, 1898, the historic courthouse had become the center of Placer County government as well as the area's best-known landmark. Age and use had taken their toll, so plans

Left: The oldest home in Auburn, the Bernhard House, was used as a private residence and a farm, and is used today as part of the Placer County Museum. Courtesy, **Auburn Journal**

In addition to being the area's main library, the Auburn/Placer County Library on Nevada Street is also used as a meeting place for area groups and organizations. Courtesy, **Auburn Journal**

were formulated in the mid 1970s for the restoration of the building. By 1978 the courts and county offices had moved from the structure, and work had begun to bring the building up to modern earthquake standards.

Restoration and preservation of city and county buildings were in high gear during 1987. Along with approving the courthouse the voters of Auburn approved a bond issue that would restore the old Lincoln Way School and make it into a community government center. The bond issue passed the necessary two-thirds of the vote requirement established by California's Proposition 13. The old school was being used for a school administration center since it had failed to meet earthquake standards as a school. Completion of the community center project is expected by 1989.

Early efforts to pay for the restoration work resulted in the formation of the Placer County Courthouse Committee. A number of fundraisers began to build up the treasury. When the structural work was completed, Lardner & Lardner Architects and Associates drafted plans for the final restoration work and the return of the Placer County Superior Courts to the building. State funding was made available through grants, and work continued into 1988. In addition to the courts, the first floor of the building will be used for a county museum.

Chapter
VI

Leaders, Folks, and Scoundrels

A small gravestone tucked away in the corner of the Odd Fellows Cemetery on Fulweiler Avenue carries a brief message: "Rattlesnake Dick, 1833-1859, Richard H. Barter, early day resident of Rattlesnake Bar, famed as the outlaw Rattlesnake Dick, fatally wounded in a gun duel with the law July 11, 1859 near the Martin Park Fire Station in Auburn."

Rattlesnake Dick, whose life was cut short by an accurate Auburn deputy with a six shooter, was a person far removed from the family atmosphere that now surrounds Auburn and Placer County. He was just one of the hundreds of interesting, unique, and colorful characters that walked the same streets walked by today's residents.

While Auburn and Placer County were still in their infancy, survival depended on one's wits and courage. Nonetheless, at the same time Rattlesnake Dick and his gang were plundering the foothills, the gentle qualities of Eulalie, "the Poetess of Auburn," were being recognized by the miners scratching a living out of the earth. The gravestones of Eulalie and Rattlesnake Dick can be found side by side in the old Auburn Cemetery, and some say the two were acquainted.

Gold was an equal opportunity attractor. People came to Auburn from around the world. Race, culture, and age made little difference to those seeking to make their fortunes with that one big gold discovery. In addition to the Indians a traveler passing through the area was likely to find conclaves of Mexican, Chinese, black, English, French, Scottish, German, Irish, Jewish, and Italian people. A few from each of these groups would settle in Auburn when the gold ran out. Most left, but those who remained formed the beginnings of a culture that survived by will alone.

Those who became outlaws found that justice in the foothills during the early years was dispensed at the end of a rope. While they are hardly citizens to be remembered with civic pride, they did capture the attention of those who recorded Auburn history.

RATTLESNAKE DICK

Richard Barter's early life gave no indication of the fate that awaited him in California. He arrived there in 1850 with his sister, Harriet Barter, and his cousin, John Cross. Richard had been raised in Quebec, Canada, where his parents were well-educated and respected members of the community. For 17-year-old Richard and his older sister, the first big change had come with the death of their parents. Their protected and cultured lives were dramatically altered, and they chose to travel to California in hopes of striking it rich in the California gold fields.

Not long after they arrived by steamer in Sacramento, the three young travelers began the trek east into the foothills of Placer County. At Rattlesnake Bar Richard Barter staked his claim. Finding a half-built,

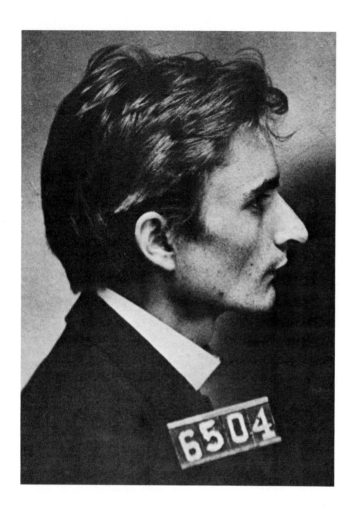

Rattlesnake Bar, seen in the center, on the Middle Fork of the American River, is where Rattlesnake Dick filed his first gold claim. Courtesy, Bob Elder

Twenty-two-year-old Adolf Weber was hung at Folsom Prison in 1906 for the murder of his family. Courtesy, Joe Campoy

abandoned cabin, Barter, Harriet, and Cross finished the structure and began to mine gold. Unfortunately Barter's life was soon to change again. Rattlesnake Bar had grown as more miners moved into the area. It had a few stores, a saloon, and a small jail. Except for gold strikes, little happened to cause excitement, but one event would have a major impact on Barter.

It began when Sam Isaac's dry goods store was robbed. Even though Auburn Sheriff Sam Austin attempted to find those responsible, after a few days all was back to normal in Rattlesnake Bar, except for Isaac, who continued his search for the robbers. Casting a suspicious eye on all newcomers, Isaac became obsessed with the crime.

Upon returning from San Francisco Barter was confronted by Isaac. Isaac claimed that Barter's new coat was one of the stolen items. Despite Barter's protests he was jailed on robbery charges. After 12 jurors had been selected, the trial got underway the next day at Dutch Jim's saloon. Within a short time Barter and his legal representative, Ben Myers, were able to show that the coat in question had been made in San Francisco and that Isaac's store had never had such a coat for sale. The jury returned a verdict of not guilty.

Although he was acquitted the incident branded Barter as a troublemaker in the eyes of many Rattlesnake Bar residents. The fact that Barter was outspoken only added to his troubles, and when newcomers heard stories of the robbery, they cast suspicious looks in his direction. Barter considered leaving Rattlesnake Bar with his sister, but only Harriet and Cross moved away. Barter stayed behind to continue his search for gold in Placer County.

Above left:Historic Placer County Courthouse was built in the late 1890s. Photo by John Elk III

Above right: The statue of Claude Chana greets visitors to Historic Auburn. Chana discovered gold in Auburn Ravine in 1848. Photo by John Elk III

Left: The Placer County Courthouse stands in the distance in this view of Historic Auburn. Photo by John Elk III

Right: The Auburn Volunteer Fire Department leads the St. Joseph's Mardi Gras Parade at the top of Lincoln Way. Photo by A. Thomas Homer

Above: The Central Valley Road Association meets at the Gold Country Fairgrounds in Auburn. Pictured are some of the entries. Photo by A. Thomas Homer

Right: St. Joseph's Mardi Gras Parade brings crowds of people to downtown Auburn. Photo by A. Thomas Homer

Left: Old Foresthill stagecoach provides rides on High Street for visitors to the Bernhard Museum. Photo by A. Thomas Homer

Far left: Bicycle racers climb up Oakwood Drive during the 4th of July race in Auburn. Photo by A. Thomas Homer

Below: The Auburn Courthouse stands out against the evening skyline above Historic Auburn. Photo by George Elich

Top: Ominous fog settles in at
Lake Tahoe. Photo by Lee Foster

Above: These boats test their
power at Rollins Lake east of
Colfax. Photo by A. Thomas
Homer

Right: *Sailboats rest along the*
shoreline at Lake Tahoe. Photo
by Mark E. Gibson

Left: Vintage cars gather at the shoreline of Lake Tahoe in Placer County. Photo by Mark E. Gibson

Below: The sun sets over the Sierras at Lake Tahoe in Placer County. Photo by Mark E. Gibson

Right: Interstate 80 is seen here looking west from Penryn. Photo by A. Thomas Homer

Middle: Clementine Dam is seen here on the North Fork of the American River. Photo by John Elk III

Right: Purple lupines are scattered throughout the Sierra foothills in Placer County. Photo by John Elk III

Above left: Children and adults can ride the Apple Ridge Railroad at Apple Hill. Photo by George Elich

Above right: Clouds congregate over this Apple Hill mobile home park. Photo by George Elich

Left: Autumn trees accent this Dutch Flats hillside. Photo by George Elich

Above left: Squaw Valley in Placer County was the location of the 1960 Winter Olympics. Photo by Mark E. Gibson

Above right: These tall trees shade the fresh Sierra snow. Photo by George Elich.

Right: Early foothill memorabilia can be found at this antique shop in Dutch Flats, a five-minute drive from Interstate 80. Photo by George Elich

*Left: The tranquil beauty of
Lake Tahoe is timeless. Cour-
tesy, Placer County Chamber of
Commerce*

*Below: Old Auburn Cemetery is
where Rattlesnake Dick, famous
foothill bandit, can be found.
Photo by A. Thomas Homer*

Living alone provided Barter with more freedom
than he had ever had. Within weeks of his sister's
departure, he began frequenting Auburn saloons. His
new freedom also led to more confrontations with the
law.

On one occasion he was loaned a horse by a local
blacksmith while his own horse received a new set of
shoes. Riding out of town Barter met with
Undersheriff John Boggs, who ordered him off the
horse and accused him of being a horse thief. The
blacksmith, it seemed, had loaned Boggs' horse to Barter by mistake. After some confusion the blacksmith
explained what had happened, and Barter was allowed
to return to Rattlesnake Bar. His first meeting with
Boggs, known as one of the toughest lawmen in the
foothills, had not been a good one. It also was not the
last time the two men's paths would cross.

Some time later Barter was awakened in his cabin
by Boggs, who had obtained an arrest warrant following the theft of a horse. This time Barter stood trial.
Based on Boggs' testimony, which included his previous charge that Barter had purposely taken his horse,
Barter was found guilty and sentenced to two years in
prison for a crime he did not commit. He was released
on the date of his imprisonment when the stolen horse
was found in the possession of a Humbug Canyon resident who had confessed to the crime.

RATTLESNAKE DICK
1833 — 1859

RICHARD H. BARTER, EARLY DAY RESIDENT
OF RATTLESNAKE BAR, FAMED AS THE OUTLAW
RATTLESNAKE DICK. FATALLY WOUNDED IN A
GUN DUEL WITH THE LAW JULY 11, 1859 NEAR
MARTIN PARK FIRE STATION IN AUBURN.
ORIGINALLY BURIED IN THE OLD AUBURN CEMETERY
ON EAST STREET. MOVED TO THIS SPOT IN 1893.

NO FURTHER SEEK HIS MERITS TO DISCLOSE,
NOR DRAW HIS FRAILTIES FROM THEIR DREAD ABODE;
THERE THEY ALIKE IN TREMBLING HOPE REPOSE,
THE BOSOM OF HIS FATHER AND HIS GOD.

A narrow bridge crosses the Middle Fork of the American River leading to Rattlesnake Bar where Rattlesnake Dick first settled with his sister in Placer County. Courtesy, Bob Elder

At the age of 19 Richard Barter had been twice arrested and tried when he was innocent. He decided to move north and never return to Rattlesnake Bar or Auburn. In Shasta Barter earned a living for a short time at the gaming tables. Again fate intervened.

Upon returning to his room one night, he found he had been robbed of the gold dust hidden in his clothes. Taking his two pistols with him, he found the men he suspected and called them out. Shots were fired. One of the men fell to the ground, while the other disappeared into the darkness. Searching the wounded thief, Barter found half his gold. It was still in his pouch, which had the initials "R.B." on the outside. He was cleared of any wrongdoing, but the incident was witnessed by an Auburn resident who remembered Richard Barter. Word quickly spread through the mining camp about Rattlesnake Dick.

It wasn't long before Barter was without money, a place to stay, or a job. At that point he decided that a life of crime would be one way to pay back all those who had wrongly accused him in the past. It would also provide him with the funds to live in the style to which he had once been accustomed. The first known robbery carried out by Barter took place in a lonely ravine between Shasta and Redding.

Auburn constable John C. Boggs arrived in Auburn in 1849. Boggs became well known during the early 1850s through his encounters with the famous bandit, Rattlesnake Dick. On one occasion Boggs arrested Rattlesnake Dick only to have the bandit escape from jail. Boggs was elected sheriff of Placer County in 1879. Courtesy, Bob Elder

As he waited in the bushes Barter spotted two drummers, both returning from successful sales trips. Barter jumped from the bushes and ordered both men to turn over their gold dust. Barter, who wore no mask, looked at the two men and said, "If anyone asks who robbed you, say it was Rattlesnake Dick, the Pirate of the Placers."

Over the next few years Rattlesnake Dick's exploits became legendary. On a number of occasions he returned to Auburn to take advantage of the rich gold deposits available for the taking. From Auburn to Sacramento to Shasta, Rattlesnake Dick was known for his brash life-style and rugged independence. But as more and more lawmen began to track down outlaws, areas which had once provided a safe place to hide were no longer safe. Friends to be counted on were no longer friends. Time was running out for Rattlesnake Dick.

As if he knew he could hide no longer, Rattlesnake Dick and his friend, Aleck, took the trail leading to Auburn one hot summer day. Aleck urged Barter to turn off the trail near the edge of town, but Barter refused. Rattlesnake Dick wanted a drink at the best saloon in Auburn. Under the blazing sun the pair of robbers sat high in the saddle as they rode into the town. Only a few men were inside when they calmly entered the bar, but a crowd soon began to gather in the saloon. Inside was Rattlesnake Dick—the famed Pirate of the Placers had returned to Auburn.

As one man attempted to leave the bar, Barter reached out and grabbed the man's shoulder. "You can

tell Constable Boggs that Rattlesnake Dick is in town," he said. "Tell him if he wants me to come out and get me—but tell him to come prepared!" Boggs, however, was out of town.

That day was July 11, 1859, just nine years after the law-abiding Richard Barter had arrived in Rattlesnake Bar with his sister. Auburn had changed and so had Barter. After his drink he rode out of town on the Illinoistown Road. Word of his visit in Auburn spread like wildfire and reached undersheriffs George Johnston and William Crutcher as they were standing in front of the courthouse. Dick's reputation made it impossible for the two lawmen to put a posse together. With Boggs gone only businessman George Martin would join the two undersheriffs as they set out after Rattlesnake Dick and Aleck.

Just outside of town the three Auburn lawmen came face to face with the two highwaymen. No words were spoken, but shots filled the air. Within seconds Martin lay dead in the dust, and Johnston was wounded. Rattlesnake Dick and his partner had disappeared. Crutcher took Martin's body back to Auburn, and Johnston went for medical treatment. Johnston felt sure that Rattlesnake Dick must have been wounded. "I never miss at that range," he said. Johnston was right.

The next morning, as the Iowa Hill stage wound its way toward Auburn, the driver spotted a man sitting up straight with his back against a tree. Slowly the driver and a group of passengers gathered around the still figure with its eyes still open. Even though the Pirate of the Placers had been shot twice in the chest, he had made it to the tree. But before he had died Rattlesnake Dick had left a message for those who would find him. On a small piece of paper he had written: "Like a true Briton, Rattlesnake Dick dies but never surrenders."

MARY FEE SHANNON

Mary Fee Shannon took one of Auburn's best kept secrets to her grave. Mary arrived in Auburn in 1854 with her husband, John. The Shannons began publishing the *Placer Democrat* on April 19, 1854. Among the items on the pages of one of Placer's first newspapers were several poems written by a poetess who signed her work "Eulalie." Both the Shannons denied any knowledge of who the mysterious Eulalie might be.

Just as readers began to look forward to her poems, Eulalie's works stopped appearing. The mystery was

*The Placer County Bank, seen in
the center of this business block,
was robbed in 1904 by Adolf
Weber, who was later executed
for the murder of his family.
Courtesy,* **Auburn Journal**

solved after Mary's death. She had been brought up in Ohio and had attended the finest schools before moving to Auburn. She became pregant shortly after her arrival, and she died in childbirth after having lived in Auburn less than a year.

The Shannons lived in the Junction House, a stage stop where the road split toward Foresthill and Yankee Jim's, so Mary was buried in Auburn's old cemetery. With a large crowd looking on, her husband stood over her grave and softly said, "We have buried Eulalie here also."

Mary Fee Shannon published her book of poetry in Auburn shortly before her death. Although *Buds, Blossoms and Leaves* was written for the most part in Ohio, it gave her a place in history as the first woman to publish a book of poetry in California.

As was the case with many young couples who came to California during the Gold Rush, the death of Mary Fee Shannon was closely followed by that of her husband John. Leaving Auburn after the death of his wife, he went on to establish a number of Democratic newspapers in Northern California, only to sell them a short time later. Politics was all that Shannon lived for after the death of his wife. It was also politics that would result in his own death.

After a running newspaper battle between his own paper in Tulare County, called the *Delta*, and that of his Republican rival, William Gouverneur Morris, the two men resorted to violence. First Morris had Shannon's printing presses destroyed. Then, on November 14, 1860, Shannon charged into Morris' office and pistol-whipped the Republican editor. As Shannon turned to walk toward the door, Morris pulled out his pistol and shot Shannon, killing him instantly.

ADOLPH JULIUS WEBER

Auburn resident Adolph Julius Weber shared the fate of five other Placer County residents: all six men were hung at Folsom State Prison between 1895 and 1933. Each was executed after being found guilty of murder in Placer County. Weber's crime, however, has proven to be the most notorious in the 100-year history of Auburn.

The young Auburn resident's story ended on September 27, 1906. He was only 21 years old at the time of his death. His story began, however, early in May 1904, at the Placer County Bank on Commercial Street in Auburn. A lone gunman handed a note to the

bank's assistant cashier demanding money. Without waiting for a reply the robber leaped over the counter, took the money, and ran out the front door. Within seconds he was in his wagon and driving out of town. A posse was formed to follow the robber on the road toward Newcastle. As it left young Weber joined its ranks. Unable to find the robber the posse returned to Auburn without a clue. For the next six months the crime remained a mystery.

Weber's downfall began to take shape on November 10, 1904, when the fire bell sounded in Auburn. The home of one of the area's most respected families was on fire. Located on Snowden Hill above Auburn, it belonged to Julius Weber, Adolph's father. Volunteers were unable to slow the flames, and the structure burned to the ground. Adolph Weber joined the efforts to put out the fire.

Firefighters did manage to get inside the building and carry out the bodies of Weber's mother, Mary, and his sister, Bertha. The youngest Weber child, Chester, managed to escape the blaze, but he died shortly thereafter. Suspecting something was wrong authorities took the bodies to the morgue for autopsies. Both women had small bullet holes over their hearts. Chester appeared to have been struck by a heavy instrument. News of the triple murder spread throughout California and was carried by some international newspapers.

Adolph Weber was named as a suspect. He was known to have taken sadistic delight in hurting helpless animals. It was also believed that Adolph could have robbed the Placer County Bank six months earlier. The investigation accelerated when the body of Adolph's father was found in the ashes of the home a few days later. He too had been shot. Investigators turned their attention to a barn owned by Julius, a place often used by Adolph when he wanted to be alone. Inside the barn they found $5,500. They believed it to be what was left of the money taken in the robbery. Still missing was $800, but a trip taken by Weber to San Francisco after the robbery could have used up some of the stolen cash. During the trial that followed, experts presented evidence that the note left during the robbery was written by Weber. According to some hypotheses the young man had taken such delight in the ease of robbing the bank that he felt he could have his family's entire estate by murdering them.

This crime might have gone unsolved if it were not for two factors. The first was the absence of a gun next to Julius Weber's body, which eliminated the possibility of a murder/suicide. The second was that all the win-

Suspected as being the mysterious poetess who signed her works Eulalie, Mary Fee Shannon *and her husband lived in the Junction House.*
Courtesy, **Auburn Journal**

Facing page: The Auburn Print Shop was located next to the post office on Main Street. Pictured in the photograph, at right, is Jack Predom, owner and operator of the shop. Courtesy, The Mel Locher Collection

Above: Vern McCann, at far left, is photographed here with the Auburn Journal staff. Courtesy, Auburn Journal

Her home at the intersection of Railroad and High streets was one of the best kept up in the area. Throughout her life in Auburn she was a key supporter of any project that was for public improvement.

dows were closed before the fire started. Without a flow of air the flames smoldered for some time. Although the house was burned completely, firefighters were able to recover the two bodies, leading to the discovery of the murders.

Adolph Weber never confessed to the murders or the robbery. As he walked to the gallows at Folsom Prison, he said nothing. Since there were no witnesses, the 21-year-old Auburn man had been convicted on circumstantial evidence. His life and death, however, were front page news around the world.

MRS. H.J. CRANDALL
Historians say that Mrs. H.J. Crandall was the first non-native woman to live in Auburn. She arrived during the pioneer days, and she remained a resident until her death. She was known for her work with her church as well as for helping those less fortunate than herself.

VERNON G. MC CANN
If anyone earned the title "Mr. Auburn," it was Vernon McCann. McCann was born across the street from the Auburn Courthouse on May 20, 1900. "Mac," who attended both Auburn Union Grammar School and Placer High School, took advantage of his free time during the summer of 1914 to work for the *Auburn Journal*, which at that time was a daily publication. In those days he could earn $4 a month as a carrier. He also sold subscriptions and got $2.50 for each one he sold. After attending high school he went on to the University of California, Berkeley, for two years before deciding law was not the field he wanted to pursue.

Returning to Auburn he again joined the staff of the *Auburn Journal*. McCann worked for the *Auburn Journal* for over 50 years. He did everything from selling advertising to reporting the news.

Each year a citizen is selected in Auburn to receive the McCann Award, given to the man or woman who best displays the character of Vern McCann and his lifelong love for Auburn.

Chapter
VII

Partners in Progress

The lore of gold and its history are intertwined and forever a part of Auburn, a commnity nestled in the foothills of the Sierra Nevada Mountains.

Claude Chana discovered gold in Auburn Ravine and his name joined those of Sutter and Marshall in the annals of California's history of the search for the precious metal. As a reminder of this legacy, a giant statue of Claude Chana panning for gold greets visitors to Auburn and lures them to be photographed beside his 25-foot-tall image.

Auburn's beautiful silver-domed courthouse, constructed in the mid-1980s, is a striking reminder of its rich and interesting past. Currently being renovated, the courthouse is a landmark for all to see as they journey along Interstate 80, the broad ribbon of freeway that bisects the county and ties Auburn to western and eastern Placer County as well as to the rest of the United States.

Once called North Fork Dry Diggings, Auburn is closely surrounded by the communities of Meadow Vista, Christian Valley, and Applegate to the east, and Ophir and Newcastle to the west. Auburn, the county seat, is in the heart of Placer County, which itself is located in North Central California between Sacramento and the Nevada State line and is bordered on the north by Nevada and Sierra counties, and on the south by the American and Rubicon rivers and El Dorado County.

Auburn abounds in natural beauty, and its temperate climate provides a long growing season as well as the pleasures of the four seasons. Owing to its friendly climate, Auburn is the center for outdoor activities throughout Placer County.

Off Highway 49, just outside Auburn, the North Fork of the American River offers all types of recreation including swimming, hiking, gold panning, and rafting. Also nearby, offering nearly unlimited water sports, are lakes Clementine, Combie, Rollins, and Folsom. Looking east, one can see the snow-capped Sierra Nevada Mountains, less than an hour away by car and a mecca for a multitude of activities, among which are skiing, fishing, backpacking, and hunting.

With Sacramento less than an hour to the west, Auburn and the surrounding communities reflect the vital energy of California's political center. Its close proximity to the state capital has attracted a great number of people to this foothill community, and growth and change have become an integral part of the present and future of Placer County and of the Auburn area. As the histories on the following pages illustrate, the people of the Auburn area are ready to meet the future, yet are mindful of preserving their traditions and their rich heritage.

The organizations whose stories are detailed in the following section have chosen to support this important literary and civic project. The civic involvement of the Auburn/Placer County area's businesses, institutions, and local organizations, in cooperation with its citizens, has made the area an excellent place to live and to work.

AUBURN AREA CHAMBER OF COMMERCE

The Auburn Area Chamber of Commerce works with eight area business associations and the Auburn Area Visitors' and Convention Bureau in promoting tourism and business in the community. The chamber also works with the city on issues such as population, growth, traffic, and zoning.

In the heart of the Motherlode, an area abounding in California Gold Rush history, a group of leading Auburn businessmen gathered together in 1906 to discuss the formation of a community chamber of commerce. The stated purpose of these farsighted individuals was to have a "central body always organized and always ready to take up any proposition for the public good," and to promote business and commerce.

On August 4 of that year the Auburn Area Chamber of Commerce came into being. Fifteen members were elected to the first board of directors: Fred Brye, E.T. Robie, Senator W.B. Lardner, J.W. Morgan, F. DeGomez, A.L. Smith, B.B. Deming, J.M. Francis, W.A. Freeman, William G. Lee, J.G. McLaughlin, E.S. Birdsall, F.S. Stevens, J.F. Hodge, and attorney L.L. Chamberlain, who served as the first president.

One of the chamber's first actions was to promote better train service in Placer County, and in September members initiated a petition requesting Southern Pacific Railroad to add an extra train to the daily round-trip schedule from Sacramento to western Placer County.

The Auburn Area Chamber of Commerce was also responsible for establishing a city hall in Auburn. Meeting at various offices and restaurants during their early years, chamber members soon realized the necessity of a building where city business could be conducted. The city also lacked a fire station in which to house expensive fire-fighting equipment and trucks. In recognition of these needs, the chamber, in 1935, began working on obtaining a building.

Under the direction of well-known Auburn pioneer Wendell Robie, a building committee drew up a proposal seeking federal funding for the project. The city purchased a lot at the corner of High and Lewis streets, construction was begun, and by early 1937 the new City Hall/Fire Department/Chamber of Commerce Building was completed. The city received federal relief for 80 percent of the costs, with the remaining portion coming from taxpayers.

In 1948 the Auburn Area Chamber of Commerce became incorporated. "Throughout its history, the organization has been a sounding board to unite the business and residential communities of Auburn. Eight area business associations, as well as the Auburn Area Visitors' and Convention Bureau, work together under the umbrella of the chamber to promote business and tourism in the community," says chamber executive director Bruce Cosgrove.

With an Auburn area population of 50,000, the organization also works with the city on issues concerning growth, zoning, traffic, and population. Members have been actively involved in the Auburn Dam project; the Main Street, USA, program to revitalize the downtown area; and now a potential bypass for Highway 49.

From a handful of Auburn businessmen gathered in 1906, the Auburn Area Chamber of Commerce has grown to include more than 900 members. Today more than ever business, the public, government, and residents of the Auburn area are working together to build a better community.

After 50 years of sharing space with city hall and the Auburn Fire Department, the Auburn Area Chamber of Commerce moved to larger offices, located at 512 Auburn Ravine Road.

After 50 years of sharing space with city hall and the Auburn Fire Department, the Auburn Area Chamber of Commerce relocated to its own, larger quarters at 512 Auburn Ravine Road.

AUBURN IRON WORKS/HARRIS WELDING, INC.

One of Placer County's oldest blacksmith shops, Auburn Iron Works has been operating in the same location for a century. The shop is owned by the Harris family of Applegate, which also has owned and operated Harris Welding, Inc., in Citrus Heights, for more than 50 years.

The family industry was started by Harold Harris as Harris Welding Works in 1936. Sons Phil, Kent, and Alan worked in the shop after school. In 1941 Harold operated the business alone while the three boys were away serving in the war effort. When they came home, the family formed a partnership. They soon added a supply and rental business to the welding operation.

When State Highway 40 became Interstate 80, it was Kent Harris who used his torch to help Congressman "Bizz" Johnson cut the dedication chain during ceremonies. It was also Kent Harris who took over as owner of the welding and supply division of the business in 1953, when the family partnership was dissolved. As Citrus Heights grew, the thriving Harris Welding business was remodeled to keep abreast of the change.

Family enterprise rekindled in 1970, when Harris Welding, Inc., was formed as Kent's family corporation. Three years later Auburn Iron Works was purchased as its subsidiary.

Auburn Iron Works was established at the corner of Elm and Railroad streets shortly after the Central Pacific Railroad reached Auburn. Founded by owners Allen and Sandhorfer in 1888, the business passed through several owners before being acquired by the Harris family in 1973.

Harold Harris died in 1972, followed by Kent Harris in 1974. In a business traditionally viewed as a man's world, the Harris family operations came under the corporate direction of Kent's widow, Norma, who, up

until that time was a homemaker with four children. Taking full responsibility for both welding businesses, she enrolled as the only woman in a welding course at Sierra College.

"From 1976 until 1983 we had an all-female-officer corporation," Harris reflects with a laugh, noting that she appointed her three daughters as directors and corporate officers. "At the time my son, Kent, was still a minor and could not take part in the business," she adds.

Today all four Harris offspring are involved in managing the corporation, which has 21 paid employees. Daughter Kathleen Haupt is executive vice-president and office manager in Auburn. Oldest daughter Joanne Garland is secretary/director. Marilee Enright, the youngest daughter, now lives in Wyoming and is a director. Son Kent Harris, Jr., currently a law student in San Diego, serves as treasurer. Son-in-law Douglas Haupt is general manager. Even granddaughter Amy Supinger works at both locations during the summer months.

Active in the community, Harris is past president of the Sierra College Foundation, Golden Chain Council, Soroptimist International, the Auburn Area Chamber of Commerce, and Roseville Sons of Italy. She serves on advisory boards for welding and metals at Placer High School and Sierra College, sponsoring Kent Harris Memorial Scholarships for welding excellence at both institutions. She has also been on the 20th District Agricultural Fair Board, and is a member of Native Daughters of the Golden West and the American Legion Auxiliary. She is among those listed in *Who's Who of California Executive Women,* and is also listed in the current *Who's Who in California.* Harris was named Placer County Woman of the Year in 1985, received the *Auburn Journal* McCann Award, and was granted the Business

and Professional Woman of Achievement Award.

The corporation maintains local community involvement as well, belonging to chambers of commerce in Citrus Heights, Roseville, and Auburn.

BELOW: Norma Harris, businesswoman and community leader.

BOTTOM: Auburn Iron Works is the oldest working blacksmith shop in Northern California. It was established in 1865 on Elm Avenue and Railroad Street shortly after the Central Pacific Railroad reached East Auburn. It was designated as a state historic point of interest in May 1984. And on January 22, 1988, Auburn Iron was presented with the California Historical Society Centennial Business Award in recognition of more than a century of continuous business activity, service, and contribution to California's economic growth and vitality.

LOU LA BONTE'S, INC.

Lou La Bonte began a family tradition in 1946 when he opened his first restaurant in Weimar. A forerunner of the mini-marts found today, Lou La Bonte's first opened off Old Highway 40 as a restaurant connected to a gas station and liquor store.

"When I was a kid they served lots of hamburgers and hot apple pie with cheese on it," remembers proprietor Judi La Bonte, Lou's daughter.

Founder Lou La Bonte had been a musical arranger for 20th Century Fox Studios in Los Angeles and had driven through the Auburn area many times on his way to Lake Tahoe. He and his wife fell in love with the foothills. When his eyesight began to fail, La Bonte settled his family in the Auburn area to begin a new career in restaurant ownership.

The establishment moved to its current location off Interstate 80 in Auburn in 1955, replacing the 25-cent hamburgers and fried-chicken-in-a-basket with a continental menu featuring American and Continental cuisine.

Today the restaurant is still under La Bonte ownership, offering food and entertainment of the highest standard. And Judi La Bonte, owner/operator, who has worked with the family business since she was a child, hopes to keep it that way. Lou La Bonte's was the first dinner house in Auburn, offering not only quick service to travelers and local customers but more full-bodied fare as well. The restaurant still serves many tourists, and Judi La Bonte eagerly looks forward each winter to the snow that attracts skiers to the Sierra Nevada slopes and the La Bonte cuisine.

Lou La Bonte's has been instrumental in the expansion of both business and cultural life in the Auburn area. In the early 1940s and 1950s Lou La Bonte worked towards widening Highway 40 (now Interstate 80) to four lanes over Donner Summit. He was on the original committee to promote the Auburn Dam Project, and traveled to Washington, D.C., to lobby for Auburn's business interests. A member of the Auburn Elks Club, he sponsored various community events.

Judi La Bonte has carried on that tradition, sponsoring many local events as well as being a member of Soroptimist International of Auburn and the Auburn Business and Professional Women's Association. She also serves on the boards of directors of the Interstate 80 Association, the Auburn Area Chamber of Commerce, and the Placer Ballet Theatre Company.

She had instituted a dinner theater in the restaurant's banquet room, where an Auburn Theatre group performed weekly for several months. The restaurant also features a piano bar where both professional and amateur musicians have played, a tribute to Lou La Bonte's musical talents.

Judi La Bonte's goal is to carry on the La Bonte tradition of fine food and service through her children, Louis, age 19; Tony, 16; and Crystal, 10. She hopes in the not-too-distant future to turn the business over to them.

"I want Lou La Bonte's to continue to be one of the only independently owned restaurants between San Francisco and Reno," Judi La Bonte notes. "I'm sure my dad would be proud to see his name still up in neon lights."

R&W PRODUCTS

R&W Products settled in the foothills in 1978 as the first high-technology business in Auburn. The company develops and produces precision ceramics to custom specifications for use in aerospace, medical, and analytical and process-control equipment, and has become the largest producer of ceramic blood shear valves in the country. It is one of only 10 American companies that both develops prototype ceramic parts and manufactures them in its own plants.

Founded in 1962 in Redwood City, California, by Will Rogers, a shop machinist, and Bob Wire, an industrial engineer, R&W Products began in a garage. Product developments soon earned the partners several production contracts, and they moved into regular office and manufacturing space. When the firm had attracted enough business to require further expansion, the founders accepted an invitation from Rol Sutton, then the economic development director for Placer County, to relocate to the Auburn area. It was he who predicted that the company would prosper there. He calculated correctly, and now he serves as marketing director for the firm that came to Auburn with 12 employees and $300,000 in sales, and today boasts 115 employees and sales of more than $6 million annually.

The business was purchased five years ago by an investment group. Although R&W is a subsidiary of Fine Particle Technology Corporation of Camarillo, California, it accounts for approximately 95 percent of the mother company's revenues. President of the privately held corporation is Sten Walls, an industrial engineer.

Almost all of R&W's industrial ceramic parts are shipped outside of

R&W Products executive team. Left to right are Rol Sutton, marketing director; Chuck Brown, vice-president/operations; Sten Walls, president; Yvonne Wheatley, finance manager; and Ernie Cuff, vice-president, manufacturing/engineering.

the area to fulfill private and government contracts, yet the firm has made a definite economic impact on the community. Many of R&W's employees have been hired from the local work force, and the company continues to generate financial support for the community.

R&W Products officials worked closely with the City of Auburn to build a 19,000-square-foot plant near the Auburn Airport. Recently the firm leased part of a new 60,000-square-foot building next door to the main facility;

the arrangement will allow R&W to departmentalize the production and prototype manufacturing areas of the business. Other growth plans include expanding the market base in current service areas, refining new processes, and exploring the use of new materials to make precision parts.

R&W has pioneered a precision injection-molding technique that now makes it economically feasible to use ceramic parts in areas where they were formerly too expensive. The company has also developed high-temperature bonding systems to mold ceramics to ceramics and join ceramics to metals in innovative ways.

In offering to the industrial high-technology marketplace highly intricate ceramic parts adaptable to a variety of uses, R&W Products is also helping potential customers avoid high research and development costs involved in creating custom pieces.

Precision machines make prototype parts at R&W Products.

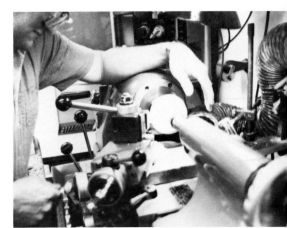

R&W products are computer inspected.

McLAUGHLIN FORD SALES CORPORATION

Located at the busy corner of Highway 49 and Luther Road in Auburn, McLaughlin Ford Sales Corporation's showrooms afford a prime view of Placer County's rapid and continuing growth in population, trade, and industry. In their years as Auburn business-people, owner and president Mike McLaughlin and his wife, Joyce, have uncovered some of Auburn's automotive history and invested in its future.

McLaughlin, a native of Nevada, Iowa, came to Auburn in 1962 to buy

Shown standing in front of the McLaughlin Ford Sales building at 858 High Street in Auburn are salesman Bud Gannow (right) and Auburn businessman Gene Dahlbert. Photo taken in 1962.

On June 1, 1962, Mike McLaughlin (right) realized his lifelong dream of owning his own automobile sales business when he purchased the Ford, Mercury, and Jeep dealership from former owner Ray Shull (left) in Auburn.

the Ford, Mercury, and Jeep dealership from former franchise owner Ray Shull. The purchase fulfilled a long-time dream for McLaughlin, who had aspired to own his own automobile sales business since entering the field. A graduate of the University of California at Berkeley with a bachelor of science and a master's degree in accounting, McLaughlin began his career with a San Francisco accounting firm that handled a number of automotive clients.

By the time he became a CPA, McLaughlin had served five years in the U.S. Navy and married his wife, the former Joyce Platt, who was born in Dunsmuir, California, and raised in Roseville. She is also a graduate of the University of California, Berkeley, with a bachelor's degree in speech and drama. The McLaughlins met at Berkeley while Mike was waiting tables at her sorority. Their daughter, Joyce Anne, was born in Long Beach during McLaughlin's years in the Navy. Their son, Craig, was born in San Jose, where McLaughlin had his first job at an auto dealership in 1945.

McLaughlin worked four years as office manager at San Jose Ford, then moved to manager at a Lincoln-Mercury dealership in Salinas under the same ownership.

From 1951 to 1955 McLaughlin resumed accounting, establishing a CPA firm in Sacramento with a partner. The automotive field was his first love, however, and McLaughlin accepted an offer from his previous employer to manage a Las Vegas auto dealership, where he worked until 1961 when he purchased the Auburn Ford franchise.

On June 1, 1962, McLaughlin moved into the Ford dealership, then located at 858 High Street on the corner of High and Reamer streets. The office was, in the words of Joyce McLaughlin, "Quite an experience." The roof leaked in the winter, so employees had to cover their desks with plastic before they went home in case it rained! During summer months, "there was plenty of fresh air and sunshine from above," she says. A remodeling project repaired the roof and added small booths for the four salesmen. Employees pitched in to help paint the refurbished facility.

McLaughlin managed the business, employing two office workers, a service manager, four mechanics, a parts manager, and one parts assistant. But there still remained a few minor flaws in the establishment. One office machine was so ancient no one could figure out how to use it. The auto showroom held only two cars, barely allowing room enough to open the doors. Lack of parking space meant both new cars and those waiting to be serviced had to park on the street until a small lot on Highway 49 and Chana Drive was finally leased to park new and used cars.

In 1963 McLaughlin Ford was selected to deliver all Jeep vehicles used on the American River project,

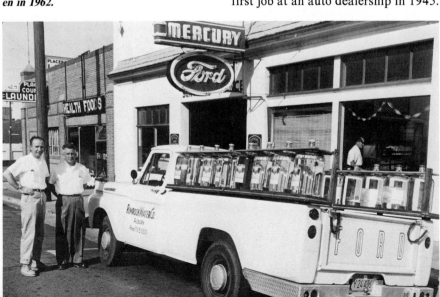

as well as provide repairs and service for the fleet.

At that time McLaughlin hired Dow Lewis, formerly of Montana, to act as office manager for the company. He is now general manager and vice-president of the McLaughlin Ford Sales Corporation.

McLaughlin's growing company needed new quarters and found them in 1966, when construction on the firm's current facility began. Relocation to the new site took place on a weekend because employees, families, and friends wanted to help, and the dealership was open for business as usual the following Monday. In the process of packing and moving McLaughlin personnel uncovered auto parts dating back to the Model T Ford, a car in production from only 1908 to 1928.

McLaughlin Ford Sales has continued to grow. Three remodeling projects have added to the original facility. The business now features 20 service stalls, conference and training rooms, and managerial offices. The dealership can park 150 cars on the property and still accommodate its 60 employees with ease.

Many of McLaughlin's original staff have stayed until retirement.

McLaughlin Ford Sales Corporation's lot and building as it looks today. After three remodeling projects, the business now features 20 service stalls, conference and training rooms, and managerial offices. The dealership can park 150 cars on the property and still accommodate its 60 employees with ease.

Longtime employees Harry Kawahata and Walter Hobbs still drop by to visit. Kawahata works on electrical jobs upon request and also keeps the company service manuals up to date.

The principals of McLaughlin Ford Sales and their families have taken an active part in the community. McLaughlin has served as president of the Auburn Rotary Club and Auburn Valley Golf and Country Club. He has been both president and treasurer of the Auburn Motor Car Dealers Association, and was elected to two three-year terms as a member of the Ford Dealers Advertising Association. He belongs to Roseville Masonic Lodge, Reno Kerak Shrine Temple, and Auburn Elks Club.

Joyce McLaughlin was an active member of the Placer High School Parents Club and has been an active golfer at Auburn Valley Golf and Country Club where she held positions in the Auburn Valley Women's Golf Association including captain. She also served a five-year term on the board of directors of the Women's Golf Association of Northern California and served as president.

Lewis serves on the board of directors of the Auburn Area Chamber of Commerce and on the Auburn Airport Advisory Committee of the Auburn City Council. He is a director of the Northern California Motor Car Dealers Association.

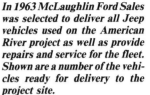

In 1963 McLaughlin Ford Sales was selected to deliver all Jeep vehicles used on the American River project as well as provide repairs and service for the fleet. Shown are a number of the vehicles ready for delivery to the project site.

McLaughlin Ford Sales has received numerous awards from the Ford Motor Company for outstanding achievements, and the dealership has been designated the AAA service facility in the Auburn area. To keep in step with the county's rapid business and population growth, all departments of the firm use the latest computer equipment in their work.

Craig McLaughlin worked part time at the dealership while a student at Placer High School, where he was on the golf team. He also served as master councillor of the DeMolay. He entered the U.S Marine Corps in 1966, later graduating from the California State University, San Diego, with an accounting degree. After passing the CPA examination, he enrolled in McGeorge School of Law in Sacramento, and is now an attorney in La Jolla, serving clients in the automotive business as well as estate planning, retirement programs, and ERISA accounts.

Joyce Anne McLaughlin attended high school in Las Vegas where she was Honored Queen of Job's Daughters Bethel #1. She also studied at the University of Oregon. She now owns a business in Solana Beach with her husband, Jim Petruk, where she is still active in the Job's Daughters organization.

RALPH M. WILSON ACCOUNTANCY CORPORATION CERTIFIED PUBLIC ACCOUNTANTS

Ralph M. Wilson founded his public accounting firm in 1975, and he says Auburn had only a handful of Certified Public Accountants at that time. He recognized a community need and opened his office, determined to offer public accounting services of the highest standards.

Wilson and his family had moved to Auburn in 1972, and his decision to start his own accounting business came after three years of commuting between Sacramento and the foothill community. When he began his CPA practice, Wilson had no existing clientele. "I just opened the doors, with no clients," he says with a laugh. "It was difficult at first, but the business grew rapidly."

For the first nine months Wilson worked alone in an upstairs office located in the Gold Country Mall on Lincoln Way. As business grew he hired a secretary, and soon moved to larger quarters in the Langwith Building on Palm Avenue.

Wilson's business was threatened with fire while he was in his first office, and though he did not lose any files, it

In November 1982 Ralph M. Wilson Accountancy Corporation moved to its present 3,000-square-foot building at 564 Auburn Ravine Road.

was a frightening experience. As a direct result he had a large, fireproof vault constructed in his present building.

In November 1982 Ralph M. Wilson Accountancy Corporation moved to its present site at 564 Auburn Ravine Road. The 3,000-square-foot building Wilson owns contains ample space for

Ralph M. Wilson, founder of Ralph M. Wilson Accountancy Corporation. Today he and his staff provide services ranging from financial statements, bookkeeping, and tax planning and preparation, to estate trusts, partnerships, and corporations.

his accounting operation and staff. His CPA practice includes financial statements, bookkeeping, tax planning and preparation, financial planning, estates trusts, partnerships, and corporations.

Wilson is diligent in keeping abreast of changes in public accounting information. Out of the 26,000 CPAs in California, Wilson was among the first 250 to complete a course in personal financial planning in 1986 offered by the California Society of CPAs and, although required by the CPA profession to attend 80 hours of continuing education in a two-year period, he often attends more than 200 hours. "We are constantly seeking better ways to serve our clients," he explains, "and I make it a point in my practice to keep as current as anyone can be."

A CPA for 20 years, Wilson received his professional status in 1967 following graduation from California State Polytechnic University in Pomona. He has spent the majority of his career in public accounting, gaining his initial CPA experience with Ernst & Whinney, an international firm of certified public accountants.

Wilson stayed with the company for four years. Prior to opening his own CPA firm in Auburn, he spent more than three years as financial vice-president and controller for a multi-corporation operation in Sacramento, with offices in three states.

An active community member, Wilson belongs to the Auburn Area Chamber of Commerce, is a past president of the Auburn Host Lions Club, and is a former member of the Ophir Elementary School Board. He is on the Sierra College Accounting Advisory Committee, is trustee and past treasurer of the Auburn Faith Community Hospital Foundation, and serves as chairman of his church finance committee.

CHAMBERLAIN, CHAMBERLAIN & BALDO

Shown here is the long brick building on Commercial Avenue called Lawyers Row in which Louis Lee "L.L." Chamberlain established his law practice in 1887, followed by his son, T.L. Chamberlain, in 1913. This building, though unoccupied, can still be seen in historic Auburn.

T.L. Chamberlain, seated on the far right, is pictured with his two sons, Paul, seated also, and Ted, standing in back, following a community gathering in Auburn. The brothers passed the California State Bar and joined the family law firm in 1950/1951. Paul is the last Chamberlain practicing law, since both his brother and father have passed away.

The Chamberlain legacy in California began in the 1840s with Thomas Chamberlain. Although he was not an attorney, he was involved in early politics and California State Legislature policy making. It was during the gold rush days that he received a homestead grant and began the Chamberlain Estate Company and ranch, raising cattle and farming approximately 2,200 acres of grain and rice between the towns of Lincoln and Sheridan.

His son, Louis Lee "L.L." became a lawyer in 1887 and established his law practice in the long brick building on Commercial Avenue in historic Auburn called Lawyers Row.

He purchased this building in co-ownership with lawyers Tabor and Slade, although he operated his firm as a single practitioner. L.L. was admitted to Placer County Superior Court in 1887 and was appointed to the Supreme Court of California the following year. He served as Placer County district attorney from 1892 to 1898. Thus, L.L. started a tradition of Chamberlains in the legal field that continues today, more than 100 years later.

L.L. Chamberlain was in court for the Adolph Weber murder trial, a precedent-setting case that helped establish the groundwork in the use of circumstantial evidence in California courts.

Of L.L.'s three sons—Lee, Thomas, and T.L.—all of whom were lawyers, T.L. took over the family law firm in 1913, the year his father died. In 1919, when the new Bank of California Building at 874 Lincoln Way was completed, T.L. moved the practice there, and it remains in the handsome, historic building in downtown Auburn today.

T.L. "Lou" had two sons, Ted and Paul, both of whom passed the California State Bar and joined the family law firm in 1950/1951. Although T.L. had had associates in the firm, his sons were his first partners, and working together they retained the name of Chamberlain and Chamberlain even though there were three Chamberlains practicing law there.

The business name was changed to Chamberlain, Chamberlain & Baldo in 1981 after Russell Baldo, who joined the firm in 1974, became a partner.

During their more than 100 years in Placer County, farming and practicing law, the Chamberlains have been active in community affairs. T.L. was a member of the Native Sons of the Golden West, California Pioneers, Masons, The Tahoe Club, and the Rotary. Paul Chamberlain has carried on the family tradition, and he currently serves on the Executive Committee to Preserve the Courthouse for the Courts.

Today Paul is the last Chamberlain practicing law, since both his brother, father, and uncles have passed away, and his children have chosen other professions—although the name will continue in the annals of legal history of Placer County.

BERTRANDO & ASSOCIATES

Bill Bertrando, broker, is president of Bertrando & Associates Real Estate. His two philosophies in business are to give clients the same professional treatment they would expect from a doctor, lawyer, or accountant, and to provide a positive work environment for the people in his firm.

Bill Owens, general manager of Bertrando & Associates and a member of the Bertrando Hall of Fame.

From its beginnings as a gold rush town, Auburn has attracted people who want a better way of life. Bertrando & Associates was founded on this principle. On July 1, 1977, Bill Bertrando and his wife opened their real estate office in the attic of 1141 High Street. Their goal was to give clients the best in professional service.

A realtor in Santa Barbara before coming to Auburn in 1975 to work for a local real estate firm, Bertrando felt that clients deserved the same personalized service he had offered in his Southern California job.

"In Santa Barbara I was selling tract homes. I didn't have to worry about sewers, surveys, or water ... I just sold homes. In the foothills, you have to know everything about land. Can you put a septic system on that

land? Where is the water coming from? What type of water is it? Can you split the land? A person has to know more about real estate in this area than in any larger cities," Bertrando points out.

The realization that there was so much to learn came as a surprise to the newly transplanted realtor. Today Bertrando has a comprehensive training program, one of the most extensive in Northern California, and agents who have excelled in certain areas of real estate in past years are selected to teach courses on selling, showing homes, time management, and goal-setting. To further educate agents, Bertrando invites professionals in to teach classes in their respective areas of expertise, such as title and escrow, financing, and newspaper advertising. Bertrando believes that new agents emerge with a better understanding of how to deal with every facet of a real estate transaction.

Bertrando's view that "it's the people in the company that make the com-

pany, not me," is a major element in the success of his business. Many Bertrando agents are Auburn natives. Most staff members have worked with the agency for five years or more, and many are original personnel. Few realtors leave the firm for greener pastures, and those who do generally form companies of their own.

Top Bertrando agents may be nominated to the honorary Hall of Fame, a roster now occupied by 11 staff members. Agents must have worked with the firm for at least three years and have accrued at least one million dollars of real estate sales for three consecutive years to qualify. They are elected to the Hall of Fame by a secret ballot of current members. Bertrando began the honor by appointing one agent per year to the position. He then selected two each year, and now lets the agents themselves participate in the selection process, which results in at least one or two new agents becoming Hall of Fame members every year.

From a staff of 10 Bertrando's office has grown to 54. In 1980 the firm moved to a new building on Elm Avenue that the realtor helped design and plan. Sales have gone from $8 million in 1978 to a volume of $51 million in 1986, garnered from 569 transactions. The realtor accomplished this status by following two philosophies: giving clients the same professional treatment they expect from a doctor, lawyer, or accountant, and providing a positive work environment for the people in his firm.

Bertrando maintains that good people make a good company by representing its founders with aplomb. To accomplish this expertise, his office offers a specialized training program for its agents, whom he believes need more knowledge than real estate salespeople in large metropolitan areas due to the nature of the foothills terrain.

Bertrando sets a good example for

Right: Bertrando & Associates began its real estate business in an attic office on High Street in Auburn in 1977. Owner Bill Bertrando opened his office to offer clients the very best in personalized service and professional real estate transactions.

Below Right: Bill Bertrando helped design and plan the firm's new building on Elm Avenue, which the company moved into in 1980. Beginning with a staff of 10, Bertrando's office has grown to a staff of 54. Sales have also risen, from $8 million in 1978 to $51 million in 1986, garnered from 569 transactions.

his staff. A graduate of the Realtor Institute, which is sponsored by the National Association of Realtors, he was the first realtor in Placer County to achieve the status of certified residential specialist under the auspices of the same association, and is one of the few realtors in the county to hold this title.

Bertrando was also the first Auburn realtor to be named a certified broker/manager by the national group, and is still one of only two in the county so qualified. His firm belongs to the Board of Realtors, and Bertrando is a member of the Placer County Board of Realtors under the National Association of Realtors.

Bertrando & Associates has made important contributions to the community, and supports youth and athletic organizations as well as the local arts scene. The firm has been a trendsetter both in business and in real estate in the county.

Bertrando studied the Auburn area carefully to gauge the growth potential of the now-booming foothills, and he has never been disappointed in its prosperity. Bertrando guessed correctly that the real estate business would flourish in coming years.

"We're growing now—we have always grown," says Bertrando, adding that he has seen many changes in both residential and commercial real estate since he arrived, and expects the field to continue to multiply in business transactions.

With creative advertising, tremendous growth, superior training, and a professional attitude, Bertrando & Associates continues to be a leader in the

foothills real estate industry. Bertrando believes that he has been instrumental in changing both standards and attitudes of realtors throughout Placer County.

Bill Bertrando values his competent staff and relies on them to maintain the firm's excellent reputation. His attention to responsible training methods and client satisfaction reflect this attitude.

WALKER'S OFFICE SUPPLIES

Walker's Office Supplies is a family business that, like a true family, has grown and changed over time, producing offspring of its own. Today the business that its owner calls "very successful" has four locations, 36 employees, an outside sales and delivery staff, and is one of the largest office supply stores in Northern California.

Purchased by Gordon and Nellie Walker in 1963 from former owner Duane Laughlin, the business began in a tiny shop at 826 Lincoln Way, offering a small selection of office supply goods. In 1968 the Walkers purchased Douglas Drugs, a shop down the street in the historic Masonic building. Nellie worked at the drugstore while Gordon continued to run the office supply business. In 1969 they enlarged the office supply store, knocking out one wall and taking over the space formerly occupied by longtime Auburn business owner Lydia Rogers, who moved her establishment, Lydia's Fabrics, to a shop space nearby. The Walkers closed out the drugstore and consolidated their remaining business, displaying greeting cards and gifts on one side of the newly expanded office supply store and arranging office goods on the other.

A year later current Walker's owner Steve Anderson came to work for his grandfather as an outside salesperson. Anderson began the job of soliciting orders from local offices and firms. His work in arranging for deliveries and offering personalized services to clients helped establish the outside sales business that now accounts for a large part of the firm's revenues.

In 1974 Gordon Walker decided to partially retire from the business. He sold 25-percent ownership of the office supply store to his grandson. Anderson ran the operation when his grand-

Walker's Office Supplies began in a tiny shop at 826 Lincoln Way in 1963, offering a limited selection of office supplies. The first of three Auburn area locations, this store currently occupies 7,000 square feet and employs six full-time personnel.

father was out of town, assuming full responsibility for six employees, including himself; bookkeeper Jenny McDermott, who started with the Walkers at Douglas Drug in 1968; three sales clerks; and a store manager. Anderson purchased the remaining 75 percent of the business in 1978 and decided to open a second location at Bell Road and Highway 49. Outside sales had helped the business to expand, and the development of trade along Highway 49 and toward Auburn Faith Community Hospital brought more business to the office supply store.

In 1982 Steve and his father-in-law, Bud Meyer, found something they wanted to purchase: a building on Highway 49, then owned by Calvin and Selby Bearry. "We moved the second store there, and it has been very successful. We moved all our bookkeeping up from 826 Lincoln Way to the Highway 49 location and expanded the downtown store's art department upstairs," Anderson explains.

But the business proprietor did not stop there. Continuing to see the need for the services of his firm in the growing community and surrounding areas,

Anderson opened a third location of Walker's Office Supplies in Grass Valley in 1986. Anderson did so by purchasing the business that had been one of his competitors there for 15 years, Action Office Supply. Recently Walker's has opened a second location in Grass Valley. In keeping with the family name of Walker's, Steve's brother, Mike Anderson, now runs the Grass Valley operations.

Many Walker's Office Supplies employees have enjoyed long careers with the business. Jenny McDermott stayed with the firm for 23 years until her 1986 retirement, but left behind a legacy: Her daughter, Kathy Tadlock, who has worked at Walker's downtown location for 12 years, currently is purchasing agent. The downtown store is

In 1969 Gordon and Nellie Walker expanded the business by taking over the space formerly occupied by Lydia's Fabrics. In the process they also expanded their inventory, displaying gift items and greeting cards on one side of the store, and tastefully arranged office supplies on the other. This store currently employs 12 people.

Walker's Office Supplies in Grass Valley was opened by owner Steve Anderson in 1986 by purchasing the building that had housed the business of one of his competitors—Action Office Supply.

run by Kass Deal, who has been with the store since 1977. Louise Prewitt joined the sales force in 1974, and Diane Barker is currently running the Highway 49 store.

Anderson says he has watched the Auburn area change as his business has grown. A town that used to be divided, in commercial terms, into Old Town Auburn and Downtown Auburn, now has a third district of trade: North Auburn on Highway 49. "North Auburn is really growing. Now it's Old Town, Downtown, and North Auburn. Some of my customers don't even know about our downtown store," he says. Anderson smiles when he remembers a concern voiced by his grandmother, Nellie Walker, who wondered if the business could support herself, her husband, and her grandson's family. "I look back on that statement and think about how Walker's Office Supplies now employs 36 people plus myself." Anderson has two sons who may someday be interested in entering the family

business.

The members of this family-run organization have been very active in Auburn's community affairs. Walker and Anderson both have been strong participants in the Downtown Merchants' Association. Anderson is a past member of the 20/30 Club and a former member of the board of directors of the Auburn Area Chamber of Commerce. Walker's Office Supplies has been a strong supporter in many community events. And while his outlook on business has changed as his firm required more people, more organization, and more coordination, Anderson continues his grandparents' promise to offer "a fair price and the best service possible."

AUBURN FAITH COMMUNITY HOSPITAL

Established in 1966, Auburn Faith Community Hospital has twice been renovated, more than doubling its acute-care patient capacity, upgrading equipment, and offering additional services. Shown in this photo is the newly completed front entrance.

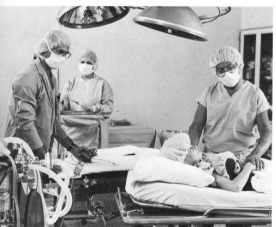

A young patient is ready for surgery in Auburn Faith Community Hospital.

In 1966 ten physicians established Auburn Faith Community Hospital, a 48-bed acute-care institution dedicated to serving the health care needs of the Auburn area's growing population. The 20 years since its opening have brought great changes to the hospital. It has twice been renovated, more than doubling its acute-care patient capacity, upgrading equipment, and offering additional services.

Yet, while staying abreast of contemporary medical advances, Auburn Faith Community Hospital has also maintained a standard of care that realizes the hopes of its founders: that modern-day medical technology can walk hand in hand with personalized hospital care.

The improvements made in response to community needs were made possible in large part by community support of the facility. Originally a for-profit organization, the hospital was sold in 1973 to the newly formed Auburn Faith Community Hospital, Inc., a nonprofit organization. During that same year it was announced that Placer County Hospital would close after 120 years of serving the area. The only other local hospital, Highland Hospital in downtown Auburn, had closed in 1966. In view of its position as the only acute-care hospital in the community, Auburn Faith Community Hospital was remodeled in 1976 to add 54 acute-care beds, physical and inhalation therapy services, fully monitored intensive and coronary care units, 24-hour emergency services, and expanded laboratory and radiology facilities.

Ten years later the hospital again expanded its service limits. A second renovation, financed by municipal bonds offered through the city of Auburn, provided three new wings to house administrative and medical offices, kitchen and dietary services, an expanded community medicine department featuring a redesigned emergency facility, and a one-day surgery unit.

Auburn Faith Hospital Foundation is comprised of dozens of members whose private financial support has enabled the hospital to provide birthing rooms with a home-like atmosphere for mothers and newborns, a cardiac monitoring system, and a beautiful community courtyard where patients and visitors can enjoy sunshine and fresh air. The foundation also directs the Lifeline program, a personal emergency response system designed to let subscribers live independently while in 24-hour contact with the hospital.

Auburn Faith Community Hospital Guild is also a vital aid to the facility. Begun in 1967, the guild continues to grow in membership. Members work daily shifts in various departments. They staff the hospital's information desk, run the newly remodeled gift shop, and conduct tours. They also operate a Patient Representative program to ensure that each patient has all the information and aid he or she needs.

With programs such as these, as well as hospice group to help critically ill patients at home, and a staff of 100 physicians, Auburn Faith Community Hospital maintains a community spirit in the practice of medicine.

ROBINSON AND ROBINSON

The Robinson family has practiced law in Placer County continuously for more than a century.

The first Robinson attorney, A.K. "Kelly" Robinson, arrived in Roseville in 1870 to shear sheep for his uncle, Will Dunlap, who arrived prior to 1850. Robinson became interested in the law, was elected Roseville Justice of the Peace, and was admitted to practice law on May 4, 1887. D.R. "Bob" Robinson, an Auburn lawyer for 40 years, describes his grandfather as "one tough and colorful guy." He remembers that, long after becoming a lawyer, his grandfather was at the California State Fair where he removed the frocked coat and string tie he always wore, entered the sheep shearing competition, and won! Kelly moved his law practice to Auburn around 1888 and served as Placer County District Attorney for two terms. Each of his four sons graduated from Placer High School and studied law.

The oldest son, Kent G., who helped construct the Southern Pacific trestle over the highway near lower Auburn, became an attorney and U.S. commissioner in Alaska.

Stephen B. graduated from the U.S. Naval Academy and Georgetown University Law School to become assistant judge advocate general for the Navy. After his retirement he became Placer County probation officer.

Kelly Dunlap "K.D." practiced law for 55 years after joining his father in 1913. He became very involved in community affairs. For more than 25 years he was simultaneously on the California State Democratic Central Committee and served as Auburn city attorney. He participated in founding the Auburn Community Foundation and Placer Savings and Loan Association, and was secretary and a member of its board of directors for 22 years. He was also president of the Tahoe Area Council, Boy Scouts of America,

and a well-known Masonic judge.

John H., the youngest, graduated and studied law at Stanford University but was called to duty in World War I. Upon his return to Auburn, he entered the postal service and was assistant postmaster for 40 years. His outstanding record of community service includes being charter president (1927) and a 60-year member of Auburn Host Lions Club, first recipient of the *Auburn Journal*'s Vernon G. McCann Award as the person best exemplifying service to his city, many years as Grand Noble Humbug of E. Clampus Vitas, and counseling senior citizens. John is widely known for his Masonic affiliations, as a past presiding officer of all local Masonic bodies and as Grand Master of Cryptic Masons of California. He is also a member of the Tahoe Club, the American Legion, the Auburn Methodist Church, and the Improved Order of Redmen, and also found time to win a national rifle championship.

K.D.'s son, Bob, after graduation from the University of California, Berkeley, and its Boalt School of Law, joined his father's practice in 1947. He followed him as city attorney, serving

for 30 years, and currently confines his practice to estate planning, wills, trusts, and probate. In the family tradition, Bob has also been very active in community affairs. He is secretary for the Auburn Community Foundation, past president of the Auburn Host Lions Club, and vice-president of the Golden Empire Council, Boy Scouts of America. He is a 15-year member of the Masonic Hall Association Board of Directors. He also has a distinguished World War II war record, commanding a Navy destroyer in the Pacific at age 27.

Kelly Robinson (standing) came to Roseville in 1870 to shear sheep for his uncle. However, in 1887, after developing an interest in law, he became the first attorney in his family and also served two terms as Placer County district attorney. "K.D." Robinson (seated), one of Kelly's four sons, all of whom studied law, joined his father's firm in 1913, where he practiced for 55 years. K.D. was also very active in the community and served as Auburn city attorney.

REYNOLDS INSURANCE AGENCY, INC.

Dave Clagett is often asked why he does not change the name of the company, since he is the majority owner of the insurance agency that is no longer controlled by the Reynolds family, its founders. He is quick to reply that the interesting 85-year history of the firm is important to him.

The history he finds so fascinating began in 1897, when a grain farmer named Augustus Eli Reynolds moved from South Dakota to California, settling near Fruitvale to work in farming and in the Gold Blossom Mine. He was trained in the insurance business as an agent for New York Life Insurance Company, and in 1903 he founded the Reynolds Insurance Agency, beginning a company that has prospered ever since.

Reynolds sold life insurance for several years out of the garage of his Auburn home, a large white house formerly located on Elm Street. The house was moved when the road was widened in 1987. In 1914 he was joined by his son, Leslie H. Reynolds, and by a second son, Walter A., three years later. The brothers opened separate insurance agencies in the 1920s, specializing in casualty property insurance, while their father concentrated on life insurance.

David M. Clagett, president of Reynolds Insurance Agency, Inc.

Walter changed his company's location to an office in the State Theater building on Lincoln Way in 1932, and to the Placer Savings and Loan building in 1963. When Placer Savings and Loan built new quarters and razed the old structure for a parking lot in 1975, Reynolds Insurance again relocated, this time to the Gold Country Mall on Lincoln Way. In 1981 the firm moved to its present location at 896 High Street.

The Reynolds brothers maintained two separate agencies until 1959, when Leslie retired. Walter's son, J.K. "Ken" Reynolds, had joined the company in 1946. He purchased and consolidated both firms in 1963, when his father retired.

Today Reynolds Insurance is owned by David Clagett, who joined the business as an agent in 1966 and began to buy stock in the firm when it incorporated in 1974, eventually becoming a partner. Clagett bought out partner Ken Reynolds upon his retirement in 1984 and became the major shareholder and president. He now shares ownership of the firm's stock with office manager Ione Culver, who also is secretary/treasurer of the corporation. She has been with the agency

since 1975 and has 40 years of experience in the insurance industry.

Reynolds Insurance remains primarily a casualty property insurance agency, specializing in commercial, personal, and group insurance, with life insurance a smaller part of the business.

Over the years company personnel have offered support and leadership to the community. Walter was president of Placer Bank (now Bank of California), spending half the day as an insurance agent and the other half in the bank office. His son Ken presided over the Rotary Club and served on the Auburn Planning Commission. Both he and current owner Clagett are past presidents of the Placer Nevada Counties Insurance Agents' Association.

Clagett is a member of the Exchange Club, past president of the Auburn 20-30 Club, and past president of the American Endurance Ride Conference. He has completed the local but world-renowned western state 100-mile ride three times.

Reynolds Insurance Agency, Inc., maintains clients of 50 and 60 years' standing. Many customers have remained even after their original agent retired. "That kind of long-term relationship is rare," Clagett says.

Ione B. Culver, secretary/treasurer of Reynolds Insurance Agency, Inc.

The staff of Reynolds Insurance poses for an informal picture in the company office.

DRIFTWOOD VILLAGE

In 1948 Ray and Beryl Thompson came to Auburn, a relatively sleepy community with little building activity. However, Highway 40, now Interstate 80, was being expanded to four lanes. It was near this section of highway at Hilltop that they built a motel and started their family—Ray III, Patty, and Rick. In the early 1960s the area from the American River Canyon to and beyond Highway 49 began showing pockets of commercial and residential growth. The topography south, east, and west was rugged. North, with its under-utilized sewer district and with highways 80 and 49, made it a logical direction for growth.

Thompson, who later became a Placer County supervisor, began constructing Driftwood Village, his housing and commercial development, off Highway 49 on Live Oak Lane in 1964.

"With completion of the freeway to Sacramento in the late 1960s and the building of a treated water system in the early 1970s, things really began to happen," Thompson says. Industrial parks, banks, and major retail and restaurant chains, as well as Auburn Faith Community Hospital, located on or near the Highway 49 corridor leading to Nevada County and along Interstate 80, toward Reno." Also, with the relocation of the Placer County Administrative Center, hundreds of county employees moved from downtown offices to Dewitt Center on Bell Road.

This area of commercial and industrial land has many noncontiguous districts governed by boards not locally elected. The city of Auburn's facilities, located outside the immediate city limits, include the Auburn Airport and Industrial Park and the sewage treatment plant.

Elected supervisor in 1968, Thompson became president of the Sierra Economic Development District (SEDD), a four-county district made up of Sierra, Nevada, Placer, and El Dorado counties. For a SEDD project NID applied for and received an Economic Development Administration (EDA), Washington, D.C., grant for a north Auburn treated water system.

The water system was sorely needed, Thompson says, since a sewer system had been authorized in 1959 and completed without a plan for treated water to complement it. Thompson is quick to point out that this three-year projection for economic growth and its accompanying jobs was exceeded tenfold after the water system was installed.

While this was happening, Thompson went before the California Highway Commission to plead his case for the widening of Highway 49. The commission agreed, and phase one was completed to the railroad underpass. Phase two was delayed for environmental reasons, although it was later funded by the EDA, Washington, D.C., from Growth Corridor funds.

Thompson laments the Bell Road Extension to Sheridan, which also, if connected to Sierra College Boulevard, would have been an ideal bypass to Interstate 80 West. A major route in the Placer County Transportation Plan, it was never built even after the rights-of-way were purchased and 100-percent Federal Aid Secondary Funding was approved. The extension was voted down four to one by the Placer County Board of Supervisors in the mid-1970s.

Now retired from political life, Thompson cares a great deal about the town he adopted. He feels strongly that the Auburn area should become one city, with locally elected and appointed officials. He is convinced the residents would have much more pride in their community if they did the planning and implementation themselves.

"With Proposition 13 in place," says Thompson, "our property tax would not increase unless approved by the voters: However, many other locally collected revenues that now go to countywide projects could be retained for local use."

Looking north from Live Oak Lane in the 1960s, Highway 49 was a recently straightened, two-lane highway. Driftwood Village property is in lower left. Dewitt State Hospital, upper left, and Cal-Ida Lumber Co., center, were Auburn's largest employers.

COHERENT COMPONENTS GROUP

The beautiful foothill landscape, high quality of life, and able work force in Placer County attracted the largest independently held laser manufacturer in the world to open a plant in Auburn in 1981. Coherent, Inc., moved the Optics Division of its international corporation from Palo Alto, California, to a 50,000-square-foot plant located near the Auburn Airport. The division primarily manufactures laser optics such as lenses, mirrors, prisms, and filters which are both fabricated and coated with thin films. The firm brought 70 employees and immediately began hiring locally.

Three years later Coherent added a Commercial Products Division to its local plant, bringing the employee headcount to 210. The Commercial Products Division manufactures laser accessories, subassemblies, and small lasers and systems. The two divisions

Two of the four planned buildings at Auburn Airport Industrial Park.

in Auburn and a subsidiary in England currently comprise the Coherent Components Group. Founded in Palo Alto in 1967 by chairman of the board, Dr. James Hobart, Coherent also operates facilities in Massachusetts, Japan, Belgium, France, England, and West Germany.

Coherent marketing communications manager Kim Woodward says the firm chose Auburn because "the labor force in this area has a high work ethic, and the quality of life here has aided

us in attracting top-notch people."

In addition, the affordable manufacturing space has allowed the company to expand into a second 60,000-square-foot building next door to the original facility. Coherent's master plan calls for four buildings on its site by 1994. The thriving operation has more than quintupled in size since coming to Placer County, with employment of approximately 400 people.

Coherent and its employees play an active part in community life. The firm belongs to the Auburn Area Chamber of Commerce and cooperated with the city of Auburn in building the company's facilities. In addition, the firm and its employees contribute heavily to United Way for Placer and Nevada counties. Coherent donated an ophthalmic laser system, manufactured by the firm, to Auburn Faith Community Hospital. The equipment supplemented a system Auburn Faith had purchased for use in delicate eye surgeries. Employees have worked with the Placer Foothills Consolidated Fire District to organize and train an Emergency Response Team. Personnel actively participate in periodic blood drives, and employees serve on the

Lasers being used to inspect critical optical components.

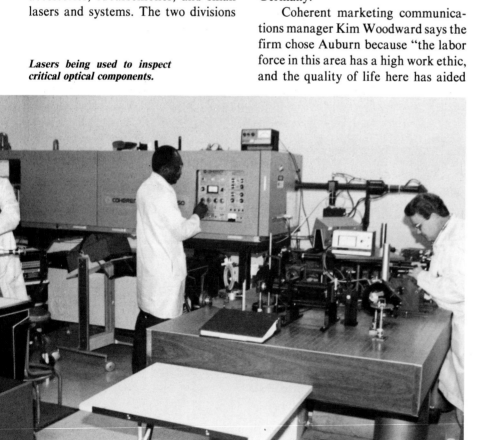

One of many laser assembly areas.

Electronics and Management Advisory Committees of Sierra College.

Coherent provides certified assembly training programs at no cost to selected members of the community, and has utilized local Regional Occupational Program students in administrative, financial, and marketing positions, many of whom have been hired by the company after completing their training.

The firm uses local suppliers and hires from the community whenever possible. In addition to superb working conditions, key benefits offered to employees include a medical policy covering 80 to 85 percent of costs, dental insurance, 100-percent tuition reimbursement, an Employee Stock Purchase Program, a 401K retirement and loan plan, and profit sharing.

Coherent has been innovative both in developing laser technology and in finding new markets and applications for its use.

Computer-controlled optical coatings equipment.

Coherent contributes a multi-million-dollar annual payroll to the community and spends an additional several million dollars each year buying materials from local vendors.

New products created by the company since moving to the foothill region include small helium neon lasers, laser power meters, a state-of-the-art YAG laser system, a laser interferometer used for precise distance measurement (with accuracy to one-millionth of an inch), as well as thin film coatings for laser optics and commercial sunglasses.

Bob Gelber, vice-president and general manager for Coherent, says, "There are only a few companies in the United States that are able to produce the quality of optics that we do. We have many highly skilled craftsmen, technicians, assemblers, and a number of highly educated engineers here. We typically have long-term employees who are able to grow with the promotional opportunities we offer. Coherent believes in moving people up through the organization as much as possible."

In an era when many large manufacturers have moved overseas in order to cut costs, Coherent preferred to consolidate in a more rural community, helping to set a trend in the manufacturing industry. And the corporation's move has been a successful one. While production costs are low, product quality and customer commitment has remained high.

With plans for more manufacturing facilities and continued research into laser technology and its commercial applications, Coherent officials expect to continue to increase the efficiency and output at the Auburn plant, using state-of-the-art manufacturing processes and equipment.

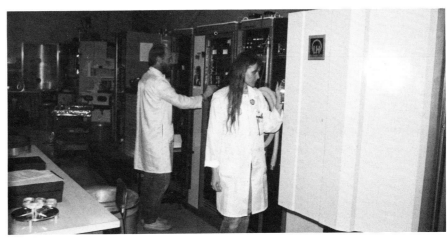

NEW CASTLE HOMES

The front office building of New Castle Homes, with the flagpole from the old state fairgrounds.

New Castle Homes is a one-year-old business settled in the tiny foothills town of Newcastle, near Auburn, on a site where home construction has been an industry since 1952.

The first firm to occupy the site was Ready-Cut Logs. Founded by Jack Peterson, the operation originally specialized in manufacturing resort-style log houses using a double-groove system. In 1970 the company began panelizing homes and built approximately 1,000 homes in the Tahoe-Sierra Nevada area.

Jack Peterson's interest in history and his involvement with the California State Fair Board led him to obtain the flagpole from the original Sacramento fairgrounds in 1978. With much effort, the historical flagpole was trucked to Newcastle and installed in front of the office that now houses New Castle Homes.

The business changed owners several times during the next years, and suffered major fire damage in 1983, when three buildings and several employees' cars went up in flames. In spite of the confusion and devastation, many employees were back on the job the following day. "The poor draftsmen! Even though their building was gone, the next day they were outside with their drafting boards, working away," remembers Betty Peterson, current bookkeeper and widow of founder Jack Peterson. Undaunted, the firm (Modular Homes at that time) began rebuilding immediately in order to keep up with production demands.

Finally, in July 1986, New Castle Homes became the newest owner of the firm. New Castle Homes is managed by Donovan Macfarlane, president, and Duane Kent, executive vice-president and secretary of Pacific Western Investments, Limited, of Nevada. The organization, which has retained 90 percent of its former employees, currently has a staff of 30 to 45 people and is one of the largest employers in the Newcastle area.

Committed to community involvement, president Macfarlane encourages company personnel to get involved. The firm joined forces with other organizations in renovating Newcastle's historical Marshall Square during the spring of 1986. Donating labor and materials, employees helped rebuild the roof of the town's gazebo. "I personally feel business has a real responsibility to the community," Macfarlane notes. "We try to participate where we can."

The firm belongs to the Newcastle Businessmen's Association, the Auburn Area Chamber of Commerce, and the Placer County Business Manager's Association.

New Castle Homes chose the seven-acre site in town to take advantage of the existing operating facilities and also its geographic location. "Our particular elevation, the moisture content of the air, and the climate provide an almost perfect combination for drying wood," Macfarlane explains. "In addition, wood can be stored here without deteriorating as fast as it might in other areas."

Unlike a modular home, which is fully constructed in the factory, New Castle Homes builds custom homes in panels that are shipped to the building site. This open-panel system of constructing the exterior siding in the factory and applying interior siding in the field came after years of evaluating various methods.

"We decided this method offers the best combination and the greatest possibility of flexibility for the custom home market, which we wanted to approach," Macfarlane says. "In our system, anything that an architect designs, we can build, and that's not necessarily true of modular and precut systems," he adds.

Macfarlane explained that factory control over quality and structural integrity is one of the primary advantages to the panel system. By using kiln-dried lumber and removing moisture, the standard configuration walls will hold their squareness longer than most houses built on the site with green wood. This system helps to avoid cracking, warping, and twisting in lumber.

New Castle Homes built and delivered approximately 40 homes during

its first year. Since most of the company's custom-built homes sell from $250,000 to one million dollars, it employs an architect and computer drafting department to design the schematics. The homes, which have mitered corners, matching joints, and leak-resistant prehung windows, are then designed by the staff architect and drawn on the computer.

The firm's Research and Development Department has worked to develop better methods for building panelized houses. One of New Castle Homes' first product developments was to change standard wall panels from four to eight feet long. "This minimizes the number of joints in a house and makes it easier to construct in the field," Macfarlane notes. "Our next

A New Castle Homes' truck loaded with house components for a custom-built panelized home.

This draftsperson is using a computer to design residences for New Castle Homes. The method is called Computer Assisted Drafting (CAD).

stage is to go to 20-foot panels, which will enable additional revisions." New Castle Homes also devised a nailing system for redwood homes that is unique in the housing industry. The wall system is flipped over and nailed from the back to eliminate much of the rusting seen on exterior panels of homes. Another building approach pioneered at New Castle Homes was to route beams and then fill in the spaces with a light material, helping to eliminate extensive nailing.

Plans are under way for expansion and growth at New Castle Homes, including possible exportation of more than 100 homes per year to Taiwan and the Orient. This endeavor would double the size of the company and increase employment in the community.

PLACER COUNTY EMPLOYEES CREDIT UNION

It was July 13, 1953, when some 30 county employees helped found the Placer County Employees Credit Union out of a desire to help themselves and their fellow workers. From an office in the Placer County courthouse, one staff member managed the operation, storing records in shoe boxes.

During the next 20 years the credit union grew from a small business into a major institution vital to the economic growth of Placer County. The firm changed locations several times until finally settling at its present location at 11460 "F" Avenue in Dewitt Center in 1973.

"We have grown from offering share savings and auto and personal loans to now offering Christmas club accounts, shares, drafts (checking accounts), certificates, and IRA accounts," says Shirley Williams, Placer County Employees Credit Union manager.

In 1971 Williams became manager. At that time the credit union had 521 members and nearly $350,000 in assets. While initially formed for Placer County employees, the organization has taken in a number of private businesses in the area and now has some 40 payrolls, including both county and private entities.

With a membership of 3,300-plus and assets well in excess of $5 million, the organization also has a branch office in Roseville acquired on April 1,

1985, when the Roseville Municipal Employees Credit Union merged with the Placer County Employees Credit Union. Through its loans the firm generates money for the Auburn community. Over the past 25 years personal loan limits have risen from $500 to $5,000.

Early in 1986 Placer County Employees Credit Union was one of two

The Placer County Employees Credit Union is run by (from left) Shirley Williams, who serves as manager, and Carol Aguilar, operations officer. Lorraine Blake (sitting) is one of the original credit union members from 1953.

credit unions in the state to be included in a pilot program that has helped create guidelines for all state auditors. Information obtained was used in establishing criteria for auditing credit unions nationwide.

Credit union members volunteer many hours to ensure the organization runs smoothly. To help keep outside costs down, a host of members serve as volunteers on various committees, such as the Credit Committee, Supervisory Committee, and Board of Directors, as well as appraisers for automobile loans. Placer County Employees Credit Union and its employees take pride in offering personal service to Placer County workers and local businesses.

Four members of the Placer County Employees Credit Union Board of Directors are (from left) E. Earl Circle, Rendell Walker, Sharon Viega, and William Hughes. Seated is Lorraine Blake, an original credit union member. With 3,300 members and assets in excess of $5 million, the Placer County Employees Credit Union has developed into an institution vital to the economic growth of Placer County.

DAVIS PRE-HUNG DOORS

The I.J. Reeves Building in Newcastle opened in 1908 as a Dodge dealership and automobile repair shop. In 1920 that wood building burned down and a concrete structure replaced it.

In the year 1908 Newcastle, California, near Auburn, saw the beginning of a new era with the opening of the I.J. Reeves Building, a Dodge dealership and automobile repair shop.

As often occurred with early-day wood construction, a fire in 1920 destroyed the building and, like most of the innovative people of that era, Reeves erected a concrete structure on the original site. The following year he was once again in business.

He eventually added gasoline pumps and a repair shop, although, according to current owners Sue and Robert Davis of Davis Pre-Hung Doors, records show that during the 1960s the Reeves Building became the site of a wood-box manufacturing company and later a sheet-metal shop. The ownership remained in the Reeves family until 1976, when the Davises purchased the building.

A licensed general contractor who specialized in building custom homes under contract for individual clients, Davis says he came to Newcastle to go into semiretirement. "I wanted to construct one house at a time using my own ideas," he recalls. "Bob always wanted to build that way," relates Sue. "Then he started looking for subcontractors and had difficulty finding pre-hung doors."

The Davises purchased the historic Reeves Building in downtown Newcastle, and their "difficulty" became a business. The pre-hung door business consists of installing interior and exterior wooden doors in wooden frames and mounting door hinges, boring holes for locks, assembling frames or jambs,

Today Bob and Sue Davis operate their pre-hung door business out of this historic building.

attaching door stops to frames, and trimming the interior casings.

"The Reeves Building itself was pretty much shot when we purchased it," says Sue. "We had to do extensive renovation, but we tried to keep as many of the old interior features as possible, such as the double doors that once opened to the automobile showroom."

Like the Reeves family before them, the Davis family could be referred to as innovative business people for the 1980s. Davis Pre-Hung Doors began as a two-person operation; the firm now employs six full-time people and has expanded to include customers from North Sacramento to Lake Tahoe.

Bob Davis never got around to building just the way he wanted to. In fact, he never got around to semiretirement; in addition to operating Davis Pre-Hung Doors, he volunteers much of his time to community projects.

He is a member of the Auburn Elks Lodge and the Auburn Area Chamber of Commerce, was the charter president of the Newcastle Area Business Association, is past president of the Placer County Contractors Association, project chairman for the Marshall Square project (a Newcastle renovation project), and was the 1987 chairman for Auburn's Funk Soap Box Derby.

The history of the Reeves Building is an important part of the business history of Placer County, and Davis Pre-Hung Doors is continuing that history.

BANK OF CALIFORNIA

Through its 100 years of backing the financial growth of Placer County, the Bank of California has accumulated a legacy that includes real wild west stories of stolen gold and a dramatic robbery. Merged with Placer County Bank in 1957, the Bank of California's Auburn office has roots dating back to 1887.

Placer County Bank was incorporated on October 31, 1887, with 1,000

Placer County Bank moved to its present location at 874 Lincoln Way in 1913. Considered one of the best small-community banking houses west of the Mississippi, its Roman Doric-style exterior symbolizes the bank's ongoing solidity and makes it one of Auburn's most recognizable landmarks.

Incorporated in 1887 with 1,000 shares of stock, the original Commercial Street office of the Placer County Bank still stands today in Old Town Auburn. Courtesy, Placer County Historical Society

shares of stock held by six prominent local businessmen: N.D. Rideout, A. Abott, D.W. Lubeck, A. Huntley, H. Neff, and F.D. Adams. The original office opened in the Lubeck Building on Commercial Street and still stands today in Old Town Auburn. In 1907 the thriving community bank acquired the Bank of Auburn, becoming even stronger.

Placer County Bank moved to its present location at 874 Lincoln Way in 1913. Designed in Roman Doric style with granite steps, metal cornices, bronze-finished lamp standards, and bronze-covered doors, the building was considered one of the best small-community banking houses west of the Mississippi. The building remains one of Auburn's most recognizable landmarks and symbolizes the bank's consistent strength over the past 100 years. The institution's interior was remodeled in 1982, retaining the charm of its history.

The Bank of California contributed to the excitement of the community's formative years—like that day in May 1904 when Adolph Weber committed the bank's first and only robbery, or when a gold collection purchased by the bank was later found to

be stolen from two Foresthill miners.

In 1937 Placer County Bank became a major contributor to the state's financial history by shipping more gold to the San Francisco Mint than any other bank in the state. The scales that weighed all that gold are currently displayed in the Bank of California Museum in San Francisco.

The Bank of California is proud of its colorful history and has preserved some of the artifacts of the past, including hand-posted ledgers dating back to the incorporation of the bank, and Adolph Weber's guns, disguise, trial transcripts, and the rope used for his hanging. Other memorabilia include shotguns used by officers as "insurance" prior to FDIC.

The institution has always been a strong supporter of the Auburn community, committing money, time, and personnel to youth programs, service clubs, and numerous civic activities. Active involvement in the community was a policy stressed by past managers, including Harry Rosenberry, Charles Haydon, and Paul Ross.

Current vice-president and manager Bob Evers states, "Another of the bank's outstanding features is the knowledge and level of service our employees are able to provide based on their average 15-year experience with the bank."

A 38-year employee and assistant vice-president, Gloria Cavenee treats clients with uncommon concern and professionalism, noting, "Old Auburn family names that appeared in our early day ledgers are still familiar." Cavenee also states, "The Bank of California is also unique in that we are the only tri-state-chartered bank with offices in California, Oregon, and Washington." In 1983 Bank of California was purchased by Mitsubishi Bank, further strengthening the institution and its ability to provide excellent service to the Auburn community.

FALCONI & ASSOCIATES

Falconi & Associates is a civil engineering partnership established in Auburn in 1975 by John P. Falconi, William J. Falconi, and Brad Langner.

Langner met William Falconi, an engineering instructor at the time, when he enrolled in Falconi's advanced surveying class at Sierra Community College. The two became friends and began doing lot surveys, parcel maps, and perks tests as a sideline to their normal jobs. Within a year they had decided to establish their own firm. John Falconi, with a 23-year background in banking, joined the team, providing a perfect combination of financial planning, civil engineering, and surveying. Their first office occupied 200 square feet on Palm Avenue in Auburn and employed one person in addition to the principals. Langner is a licensed land surveyor and William Falconi is a registered civil engineer.

In 1978 they formed a general engineering company called Falconi Construction, Inc. The organization branched out into the mining industry the next year when Falconi Construction, Inc., developed the Relief Canyon Mine in Nevada. Overseeing all environmental work, permits, and plan design for the mine, the firm was involved

in the project from claim location through production. The organization still retains an interest in the mine, which produces more than 2,000 ounces of gold per month and is operated by Pegasus Gold, Inc. The firm also owns 50 percent of a hard rock gold mine in the Allegheny Mining District out of Nevada City.

In 1983 Falconi & Associates purchased historic Alpha Explosives, originally a subsidiary of Alpha Hardware Stores, founded in 1885. Alpha Explosives distributes dynamite, caps, and bulk blasting agents in Northern California and Nevada. The firm sells explosives to the two largest mines in California, as well as to 70 smaller explosives consumers.

Falconi & Associates now occupies a 4,000-square-foot building situated off of Grass Valley Highway. An enterprise that started with no money or assets now includes a staff of 23 and a yearly gross of $3 million.

The organization has completed

Brad Langner, co-founder of the civil engineering partnership of Falconi & Associates, at Relief Canyon Mine in Nevada—a gold mine that the company developed.

Co-founder and former engineering instructor William J. Falconi at German Bar Gold Mine.

With 23 years in banking, John P. Falconi—shown here at Challenge Bridge, California—is the firm's financial planner.

contracts for agencies such as the Air Force, Department of the Navy, U.S. Corps of Engineers, U.S. Forest Service, and U.S. Postal Service.

Civil accomplishments include designing professional office buildings, industrial and residential subdivisions, and structural design. Construction work includes sewers, water, underground earth work, concrete bridges, dams, and roads.

Currently concentrating on municipal and governmental consulting, Falconi & Associates is the city engineer for Lincoln and Nevada City and previously served in that capacity for the cities of Grass Valley, Colfax, and Auburn.

"Our philosophy has been flexibility. That's why we have survived," Langner believes. Active in the Auburn community, Langner is treasurer of the Placer County Contractors Association Board of Directors and has served as president, vice-president, and treasurer of the League of Placer County Taxpayers. He is currently chairman of the City of Auburn Civic Center Advisory Committee and a member of the North Auburn Municipal Advisory Council.

BRYAN'S AUBURN FLORIST

Florence Bryan and her daughter-in-law, Jeannie.

Lauren (left) and Florence Bryan purchased their tiny flower shop, now located at 1296 Lincoln Way, in 1948, operating with only one employee.

When Lauren and Florence Bryan purchased their tiny flower shop in 1948, Florence operated Bryan's Auburn Florist with the help of one employee, while Lauren continued as part owner of the shop and funeral director with the Lukens, Vettestad and Bryan Funeral Home in town.

In 1953 Lauren joined his wife in the full-time operation of their flower business. As the business continued to grow, the store was relocated again in 1970 to its present site at 1296 Lincoln Way.

Son Jeff Bryan and his wife, Jeannie, purchased the shop in August 1975, and together with their three children they are carrying on the family tradition of giving people prompt, personalized service. Born and raised in Auburn, both Jeff and Jeannie take pride in knowing customers' names, visiting with them, and providing them the freshest flowers available.

As times have changed and the florist business has grown, the usual potted plants, flowers, and funeral arrangements have made way for a variety of other items. "We have added balloons, cards, stuffed animals, silk and dried flowers, and also musical cards to our services," Jeff Bryan says.

One of the biggest trends the Bryan family has noticed through the years is the way business holidays have caught up with religious celebrations. Secretaries' Week now equals Easter Week in requests for arrangements and gifts, he notes.

Lauren and Florence's son, Jeff, and his wife, Jeannie, purchased the flower shop from Jeff's parents in 1975, expanding and updating it by stocking stuffed animals, novelty cards, and balloons. In addition to offering the freshest flowers available, their number-one priority is in giving their customers prompt and personalized service.

Involved in the local fire department, the Auburn Jeep Club, Kiwanis, Lions, and Auburn 20-30 Club, Lauren Bryan was always generous with donations of flowers, plants, and his time toward community events and service. Active in Elks Lodge No. 1691, he was widely known and respected for his countless hours spent cooking, and on one occasion, he cooked a special dinner for then-Governor of California Edmund G. Brown. The kitchen of the Auburn Elks Lodge has been dedicated in his memory.

Like his father, Jeff Bryan is also involved in the community. In 1971 he became the youngest member inducted into the Elks Lodge. He is active in the Lions and Auburn 20-30 Club, and has coached baseball. His mother was a charter member of the Soroptimist International of Auburn, and his wife, Jeannie, is active in the Auburn Chapter of Beta Sigma Phi Sorority.

Holidays find the whole family, including Florence, working with as many as 17 employees to provide customers with fresh flowers. "From a business standpoint, I feel that a flower shop provides a lot of joy and happiness in a community because of what flowers represent in birthdays and anniversaries, as well as comforting families at difficult times," Jeff states.

Lauren Bryan was a generous contributor of flowers, plants, and his time to many community services and events. He was also noted for his cooking expertise, and once had the honor of preparing a dinner for California Governor Edmund G. Brown.

JOHANSON, BUCKWALTER AND KOONS

The law firm of Johanson, Buckwalter and Koons, founded in 1983, is deeply committed to the belief that law is a profession with high public obligations and ethical standards. Following the best traditions of the law, the members of the firm have achieved national and local recognition for their expertise in the fields of real property, business, and estate planning for individual clients.

The firm's senior partner, Theodore Johanson, a University of California at Berkeley graduate, received his law degree from McGeorge School of Law. A former title company executive, Mr. Johanson is highly regarded in the legal community for his knowledge of real property law, and, with his firm, represents local banks, savings and loans, title companies, and real estate boards.

Kenneth Buckwalter, a graduate of Occidental College and Stanford Law School, came to Auburn following 12 years of successful practice in the San Francisco Bay Area. Mr. Buckwalter's practice emphasizes real estate, corporate, and business law.

Edward Koons, youngest partner of the firm, is a graduate of the University of California at Berkeley and McGeorge School of Law, where he held membership in the prestigious Traynor Society. Concentrating on commercial and property law, Mr. Koons serves the needs of both individual and corporate clients.

The members of the firm are active contributors to the welfare of the local community, serving as directors and officers of organizations as diverse as the Tri-County Unit of the American Cancer Society, the Auburn Ravine Terrace Retirement Home, the Auburn Faith Community Hospital Foundation, and the League of Placer County Taxpayers.

Members of the firm also devote their time to the improvement of the le-

gal profession. Mr. Johanson has for the past 10 years served as a disciplinary hearing referee for the State Bar Court and occasionally sits as judge pro tem in the Placer County Superior Court. Mr. Buckwalter has been active in administering a program for the arbitration of fee disputes between attorneys and clients, and serves as an arbitrator in business cases by appointment of the Placer County Superior Court. Mr. Koons also serves as a court-appointed arbitrator and accepts selected pro bono cases for clients who cannot afford an attorney.

The firm has taken an active role in the restoration of Placer County's historic courthouse. The partners see the courthouse as a symbol of the traditional ethics and values that built Placer County, and its restoration a fitting tribute to the area's heritage of law and justice.

The Auburn law firm of Johanson, Buckwalter and Koons specializes in real estate, corporation and business law, syndications, title insurance defense, and estate planning and probate law. The partners are (left to right) Edward C. Koons, Theodore L. Johanson, and Kenneth D. Buckwalter.

Lawclerks are hired on an ongoing basis from McGeorge School of Law's list of outstanding students. The firm of Johanson, Buckwalter and Koons houses an extensive law library, enabling it to better serve both clients and attorneys in the community.

The law firm of Johanson, Buckwalter and Koons is committed to giving its clients the best-possible service, thereby enhancing the quality of justice and the quality of life in the community.

HEART FEDERAL SAVINGS AND LOAN

Since 1898 Heart Federal Savings and Loan and its predecessor organizations have served the financial needs of the people in Auburn. Today, with 26 offices in 13 counties throughout Northern California, Heart Federal continues to be an important part of Auburn's history.

In 1898 E.T. Robie of the Auburn Lumber Company organized a loan company in Auburn. In 1910 members of the original organization amended the Articles of Incorporation, and the firm officially became Auburn Savings Bank. At that time it also became associated with the First National Bank. E.T. Robie became president of both

Today, with 26 offices in 13 counties throughout Northern California, and with assets in excess of $688 million, Heart Federal Savings and Loan maintains the same brand of small-town hospitality toward its customers as it did nearly a century ago.

organizations. Auburn Savings Bank became the Central California Building and Loan Association in 1926.

By 1937 the organization, under Robie's guidance, had grown considerably, obtained a federal charter, and changed its name to Central California Federal Savings and Loan Association.

Following E.T. Robie's death in 1944, his son, Wendell T. Robie, a member of the board of directors since 1928, became president. In 1978, under Wendell Robie, the organization's name was again changed—to Heart Federal Savings and Loan Association. A dynamic leader and outstanding sportsman, Wendell Robie was a historian, expert rifleman and horseman, and a member of the United States Ski Hall of Fame.

Stuart Foster, who joined the association in 1968, became a member of the board of directors two years later. Foster was appointed president in 1980 and chief executive officer in 1983.

Recounting some of the company's

history, Foster remembers that, while in his eighties, Robie helped make a Heart Federal television commercial. "He insisted the filming take place in an authentic location on the Emigrant Trail. A conestoga wagon and team of oxen were hired, and Wendell was the bullwhacker," Foster says. "He was walking beside the team when they pushed him into the brush. Wendell grabbed a horn, thinking the animal would drag him to a place where he could walk, but the ox had other ideas. He dipped his head and Wendell fell under the wagon." When the dust cleared, Robie, who had been run over, insisted on continuing even though he had a broken collarbone and several broken ribs.

Robie's old shotgun, which decorates the wall of Foster's office, is a reminder of early days in the savings and loan business. "Wendell had kept the shotgun loaded with the safety off. An alarm in the downstairs teller's booth signaled directly into his office in the event of a robbery. He planned to stand on the balcony and let the intruder have a seat full of buckshot," says Foster.

He recalls that when the shotgun was finally fired it was not by Robie in an attempt to save the "money" but by his grandson. "The curious youngster pulled the trigger, shot a hole through the bookcase, and filled several books with buckshot," remembers Foster.

"Robie never slowed down," says Foster. "The day of his death, Halloween Day 1984, he came to the office dressed in his Indian jacket to see his costumed employees, a ritual he enjoyed. He went home for lunch, took his noontime nap, and never woke up."

This pioneer spirit lives on in the annals of Placer County history and in the history of Heart Federal Savings and Loan. Nearly a century later, the once-small business has more than $670 million in assets and continues to serve Auburn with hometown caring.

PACIFIC GAS & ELECTRIC COMPANY

Pacific Gas & Electric Alta Powerhouse—it has been in continuous service since 1902. Courtesy, Pacific Gas & Electric Company History Collection

A golden heritage is shared by Pacific Gas & Electric Company and Placer County. Gold influenced the early population influx in Placer County. PG&E's heritage can be traced back to the ditches hand dug by miners to bring water from distant living streams to help wrest the gold from dry diggings.

One of the earliest companies on PG&E's family tree, and an early Placer County firm, was the South Yuba Water Company, organized in 1850. At the peak of its activities, the South Yuba Water Company operated 450 miles of ditches and canals in and out of Placer County that at first carried water to thirsty gold claims, and then water to spin generators to electrically power mining operations. The early water-powered generators also produced electricity to light some mines and then the mining camps that became the communities of Placer County today. In addition, water availability as an adjunct to power generation played an important role in establishing Placer County's agricultural industry.

In the formative years of what eventually would result in PG&E being molded from 520 predecessor companies, men bold of vision and "can do" fortitude performed feats of construction in Placer County that, for their time, were spectacular. The names of men involved are still a part of Placer County today: James Fordyce and John Spaulding, for whom Lake Fordyce and Lake Spaulding were named, and certainly Frank G. Drum, PG&E president from 1907 to 1920, after whom the local Drum Division was named.

PG&E has and will continue to contribute to the financial well-being and intrinsic values of Placer County. In keeping with its historic origins, years of electric pioneering, and steady

PG&E linemen work year-round to provide customers with power.

expansion in step with the forward march of the county, PG&E continues to plan for better ways to meet its Placer County customers' needs.

MUSSETTER DISTRIBUTING, INC.

Though the name Mussetter Distributing, Inc., only dates back to 1976, when Richard and Kimberly Mussetter purchased the beverage distributing business, the Auburn firm's history reaches back to the turn of the century.

It was during the early 1900s that Auburn businessman Walter Jacobs founded a beer-distributing business in town. Jacobs' operation flourished, and he soon established offices in South Lake Tahoe, Truckee, and Placerville. Son Jim Jacobs managed the family operation for a number of years. In 1976 the younger Jacobs sold the family's Auburn firm to the Mussetters.

Situated among leading Auburn businesses at the Auburn Airport Industrial Park, Mussetter Distributing, Inc., has experienced steady growth in the 12 years it has served Placer and Nevada counties. Initially a beer distributorship, the business now carries a variety of beverages.

Previously a district manager for Miller Brewing Company, Mussetter had sold beverages to the Jacobs' warehouse for about a year when an opportunity arose to purchase the firm. He jumped at the chance. "Historically, beer distributorships are handed down from generation to generation," Mussetter points out. "There are third- and fourth-generation people in the beer industry today, so this was an unusual opportunity for us to buy our own business."

Mussetter, his wife, Kim, and one employee began their operation in a 4,800-square-foot building on Grass Valley Highway. Mussetter began stocking a variety of beverages, becoming the second wholesaler in the nation to carry California Coolers. Today the firm carries more than 50 lines, including several brands of imported beer, wine coolers, mineral water, and juices. "People are more health conscious today than 10 years ago," Mussetter notes. "Mothers would rather their

kids drink mineral water or juice than soda pop, and lite beer continues in a steady upward growth pattern."

In 1984 the company moved into a newly constructed 40,000-square-foot warehouse it owns at Auburn Airport Industrial Park. The corporation employs a staff of 17. Representing some 500 retail licenses, Mussetter's business volume has grown more than 1,000 percent during the past 12 years.

Creating a modern showplace, Mussetter has collected valuable articles from the past. His office contains a 10,000-pound vintage 1900 safe from the original Jacobs' distributing company that required a heavy-duty, 20,000-pound forklift to move into the new warehouse.

Mussetter's large conference room is dominated by a massive 19-foot oak-and-walnut table, and a giant video screen stands opposite a lighted bar. The room is used for company meetings and video screenings, as well as serving as a meeting place for local clubs and nonprofit organizations. Mussetter is

active in many community organizations, often donating to local associations for fund raisers and benefits. A member of the Auburn Area Chamber of Commerce, he also belongs to the Auburn 49er Lions Club and is a trustee with the Auburn Faith Community Hospital Foundation.

Kimberly Mussetter has been involved as an officer with the Auburn Area Newcomer's Club and is currently president of the Patrons Club Board of St. Joseph's School, where Jason, Jennifer, and Nicholas attend.

Bottom: In 1984 Mussetter Distributing, Inc., moved into this newly constructed 40,000-square-foot warehouse at Auburn Airport Industrial Park.

Below: Richard and Kimberly Mussetter purchased their beverage distributing business in 1976. Representing some 500 retail licenses, Mussetter's business volume has grown more than 1,000 percent during the past 12 years.

AUBURN JOURNAL

Auburn's early pioneers were hungry for news and reading material in the 1800s. *The Placer Herald,* Auburn's earliest newspaper, first rolled off the bed of a huge, iron hand-press on September 11, 1852. It was edited by Tabb Mitchell, a midwestern native who returned to newspaper work when his prospecting ventures proved unsuccessful, and published by Mitchell and two partners.

Now published by The Auburn Journal Publishing Company under Brehm Communications Inc., the 136-year-old *Placer Herald* is California's oldest surviving weekly.

The *Herald* was a strongly Democratic paper, and rivaled other Democratic papers that came and went. Not until 1863 did the Republican-oriented newspaper, *The Stars and Stripes,* appear. It went through several owners until folding. A Republican newspaper continued to flourish under the names *The Placer Republican* and the *Republican Argus* until June 1914, when the Placer County Publishing Company organized, bringing forth the first issue of the *Auburn Daily Journal* on July 13, 1914. Later a semiweekly newspaper, *The Placer County Journal,* also appeared.

The two newspapers merged and began to publish weekly in 1918 as the *Auburn Journal.* In 1972 the paper began publishing twice a week, going to three editions per week four years later, and to five daily editions in 1979. Since November 1980, when the first Sunday edition was published, the paper has published six issues each week.

Ownership of the newspaper changed often. While the *Journal* has always focused on local news coverage in Auburn and eastern Placer County, *The Placer Herald* concentrates on Rocklin, Loomis, and the Sunset-Whitney areas from its offices in Rocklin. B.A. Cassidy, publisher of the *Truckee Republican,* purchased the *Journal* in 1919 and became its editor. The paper, which remained in his family until 1965 with his son William as editor/publisher, was incorporated in 1964.

The *Journal* moved from an office on Lincoln Way to its present facility at 1030 High Street in 1962, when the paper began use of the modern offset press, one of the first in Northern California. The *Journal*'s editorial, business, and production facilities have been completely modernized.

W.J. McGiffin Newspapers acquired a controlling interest in the newspaper in late 1965. This newspaper group, now known as Brehm Communications, Inc., holds controlling stock in many local newspapers throughout the West and Midwest. It acquired *The Placer Herald* in 1966. William Cassidy remained publisher until 1968, when he was succeeded by William Pfaff, who held the position for 19 years, becoming publisher emeritus September 1, 1987. The current publisher is David Lewis.

Lloyd Beggs edited the *Journal* in the 1960s until his retirement in 1972, when Helen T. Bale became editor. A. Thomas Homer, formerly the *Auburn Journal* sports editor, became editor in March 1981.

The *Auburn Journal* has received numerous awards from the California Newspaper Publishers Association during the past 20 years. It is recognized as one of the finest community-related daily newspapers in California.

Torn down in 1946 to make way for a new highway, this building served as the former home of The Placer Herald, and was located in Old Town Auburn. The Placer Herald is (since 1852) the oldest continuing weekly newspaper published in California.

KAHI 950 AM RADIO

Radio station KAHI has been an integral part of the Auburn area for more than 30 years. Since its inception in 1957, this station, at 950 AM on the radio dial, has filled the challenging need to provide entertainment, information, and local news to growing foothills communities.

In the past decade KAHI has grown from a daytime, 5,000-watt station to a 24-hour daily, 50,000-watt broadcast medium. In 1977 there was a staff of 10; today a staff of 32 operates and maintains KAHI and KHYL, the FM station.

In the early days KAHI was the only radio station in the foothills. It served the Auburn, Grass Valley, Nevada City, and Placerville communities.

"It is focusing on community events that is the very key to KAHI's success," states general manager John Buckley, who has been with the station for 10 years. "Not long ago El Dorado

Radio station KAHI began transmitting from this building on Highway 49 in 1957 as a 5,000-watt daytime station.

County had a devastating fire. At that time KAHI was still a daytime station, but we received special operating permission from the FCC to stay on the air and provide up-to-the-minute coverage on the fire reports. The news staff stayed on the air 24 hours a day to relate both the changing position of the fire and the areas of evacuation. It is emergency situations like that that help you to recognize the importance of a local radio station."

By 1977 KAHI was a well-established AM radio station. That year a decision was made to expand the KHYL broadcasting station to 50,000 watts and boost the FM signal to reach a Sacramento audience.

KAHI, with its excellent community ties and acceptance, provided the catalyst in building a strong regional FM station. "And KAHI has remained very important. Our local identity and local community involvement is something we enjoy very much," Buckley says.

KAHI plays music that he describes as "middle-of-the-road." Following a nostalgia format, much of it spans the eras beginning with the late 1940s to today's music.

The station covers all types of local news events, including board of supervisors and city council meetings. "Covering civic events is a large part of KAHI's local appeal," Buckley explains, adding that this is something not found on most FM stations. "If it's local to the foothills community, you should hear about it on KAHI."

KAHI has concentrated on community service as an AM broadcast station. Its staff members are involved in the chamber of commerce, Auburn Faith Hospital, and many civic clubs such as the Lions Club, Rotary, and Soroptimist International.

The station recently moved to newer quarters on High Street in Auburn. Also new is state-of-the-art electronic equipment in the control rooms and offices.

On December 13, 1986, Parker Communications became the new owner of KAHI. Keeping the distinctive "hometown" flavor in this broadcasting station is one of its goals. Owners Kathleen and John Parker, both broadcasters themselves, are deeply interested in the community and civic interests of KAHI and visit the Auburn stations several times a year.

PLACER TITLE COMPANY

Placer Title Company founder Leo French follows a simple business philosophy: He hires the best people he can find, pays them the best wages the company can afford, then moves out of their way—because they will do the rest. This kind of respect and reliance on employees has served Placer Title Company well.

Placer Title Company was founded in 1973. Since then the firm has expanded from its first small offices in Auburn and Roseville to 38 offices spread over seven counties. Placer Title now supports 400 employees, although the originators admit they weathered some difficult years.

A dynamic leader who always has a twinkle in his eye, French says of the recession years in the mid-1970s and early 1980s: "Sometimes the payroll was zero. We didn't even have money to pay ourselves." He goes on to explain that the reason Placer Title Company succeeded in the face of such an adverse business climate is the kind of people that helped start the firm and the philosophy that it be run as an employees' title company. "We take good care of each other, and this feeling automatically extends out to cus-

Leo French, founder and chairman of the board of Placer Title Company.

tomers."

This business theory is the basis for the corporate slogan, "At Placer Title, when you're an employee, you're part of the family, and when you're our customer, you're our guest."

French is the embodiment of caring, and his extremely generous nature is mirrored throughout the 38 branches. He always accentuates the positive. The Placer Title Company offices in turn spread this feeling with philanthropic activities and support for community events and projects.

Today president Jerry Adams runs the daily operation of the firm, leaving French free to pioneer new offices and stoke the Placer Title Company motivational fires.

Each year on approximately November 1, the date the company was founded, he holds an office birthday party with gifts and entertainment for the employees. French, who often signs notes to employees as The Phantom, keeps morale high with thoughtful original poems and limericks that are treasured by one and all.

He is also a recruiter for the firm, always seeking good potential employees. French maintains, "The history of the title company is in its people. We don't need people to be loyal to Placer Title Company, we need people to be loyal to one another and take care of each other, and we know they will take good care of the customers."

Patrons

The following individuals, companies, and organizations have made a valuable commitment to the quality of this publication. Windsor Publications and the Auburn Area Chamber of Commerce gratefully acknowledge their participation in *Auburn and Placer County: Crossroads of a Golden Era.*

Auburn Faith Community Hospital*
Auburn Iron Works/Harris Welding, Inc.*
Auburn Journal*
Bank of California*
Bertrando & Associates*
Blaylock's Inc.
Bryan's Auburn Florist*
Chamberlain, Chamberlain & Baldo*
Coherent Components Group*
Davis Pre-Hung Doors*
Driftwood Village*
Falconi & Associates
Heart Federal Savings and Loan*
Johanson, Buckwalter and Koons*
KAHI 950 AM Radio*

Lou La Bonte's, Inc.*
Bruce A. Lyon, Attorney at Law
Maki Heating & Air Conditioning
McLaughlin Ford Sales Corporation*
Mussetter Distributing, Inc.*
New Castle Homes*
Pacific Gas & Electric Company*
Placer County Employees Credit Union*
Placer Title Company*
R&W Products*
Reynolds Insurance Agency, Inc.*
Robinson and Robinson*
Walker's Office Supplies*
Ralph M. Wilson Accountancy Corporation Certified
    Public Accountants*

*Partners in Progress of *Auburn and Placer County: Crossroads of a Golden Era.* The histories of these companies and organizations appear in Chapter VII, beginning on page 99.

Selected Bibliography

Beebe, Lucius. *The Central Pacific and Southern Pacific Railroads*. San Diego, CA: Howell-North Books, 1963.

Browne, Juanita Kennedy. *A Tale of Two Cities and a Train*. Nevada City, CA: The Nevada County Historical Society, 1987.

Calhoon, F.D. *Coolies, Kanakas, and Cousin Jacks*. Sacramento, CA: Cal-Con Publishers, 1986.

Curran, Harold. *Fearful Crossing*. Las Vegas, NV: Nevada Publications, 1982.

————. *Dot, Dot, Dot, Done!* North Highlands, CA: California State Railroad Museum & History West, 1981.

Egan, Ferol. *Fremont: Explorer for a Restless Nation*. Reno, NV: University of Nevada Press, 1985.

Elder, Robert B. *Rattlesnake Dick: A Novel of Gold Rush Days*. New York, NY: Red Dembner Enterprises Corp., 1982.

Fonseca, Janet Dunbar. *Pannings*. Dutch Flat, CA: Private Printing, 1984.

Gilberg, M.E. *Auburn: A California Mining Camp Come of Age*. Newcastle, CA: Gilmar Press, 1986.

Graydon, Charles K. *Trail of the First Wagons Over the Sierra Nevada*. Gerald, MO: The Pacific Press, 1986.

Heizer, Robert F. *Handbook of North American Indians* (Vol. 8, California). Washington, D.C.: Smithsonian Institute, 1978.

Huggins, Eleanor, and Olmsted, John. *Adventures On & Off Interstate 80*. Palo Alto, CA: Tioga Publishing Company, 1985.

Hulbert, Archer Butler. *Forty Niners*. Las Vegas, NV: Nevada Publication, 1986.

Jones, Pat. *The Colfax Connection*. Chicago Park, CA: Private Printing, 1980.

Lardner, W.B. & Brock, M.J. *History of Placer and Nevada Counties*. Los Angeles, CA: Historic Records Company, 1924.

Martin, Cy and Jeannie. *Gold and Where They Found It*. Corona del Mar, CA: Trans-Anglo Books, 1984.

McLeod, Norman. *Gold, Guns & Gallantry*. Newcastle, CA: Goldridge Press Publication, 1987.

Potts, Marie. *The Northern Maidu*. Happy Camp, CA: Naturegraph Publishers, Inc., 1977.

Samson, Karri R. *Digging Up Placer County History*. Auburn, CA: Private Printing, 1987.

Signor, John R. *Donner Pass: Southern Pacific's Sierra Crossing*. San Marino, CA: Golden West Books, 1985.

Thompson and West. *Placer County*. Placer County and Oakland, CA: Thompson & West, 1882.

Index